D1106106

THE AREA KEY OFFENSE:

A New Multiple Attack

for Basketball

THE AREA KEY OFFENSE:
A New Multiple Attack
for Basketball

by Duane Ford

Parker Publishing Company, Inc.

West Nyack, New York

©1975, *by*

PARKER PUBLISHING COMPANY, INC.

West Nyack, N.Y.

Library of Congress Cataloging in Publication Data

Ford, Duane,
    The area key offense.

    Includes index.
    1. Basketball--Offense.   I. Title.
GV889.F67   796.32'32   75-5992
ISBN 0-13-043927-4

Printed in the United States of America

How This Book Can Help You

This book explains how a unique method of keying your man-for-man offense will enable you to apply the concept of multiple formations to your basketball attack.

As the title indicates, we have abandoned the traditional means of keying an offense by verbal or hand signals, and instead, accomplish this same purpose by basing our attack on a sequence of potentially "live areas" on the court. Since the foundation of the offense centers around sequential player movement in or out of these key areas, it really matters little which alignment you are in when the attack begins. This is why multiple formations are possible.

As you will see, these four basic areas are the ones most commonly occupied in many other offenses; therefore, your personnel will not be required to play any unusual positions. In fact, the offense is designed to adjust to your own player characteristics rather than having your players adjust to fit the offense. It will be shown how you can use the area keys to run your offense with one, two, or three guards, with or without the big man. You will also see how you can make the best use of your substitutes by matching the offense with their particular strengths.

The basic play in the offense can be run with equal success from almost any alignment imaginable. Thus, by simply varying your formations, you will see how it's possible to make this one play appear to the defense as an entire offense. Our standard play with options can be run from eight basic formations. This basic play and the three alternate plays with standard options, when run from the various formations described, can yield over 100 play possibilities. Add to these the free-lance options available, and you have a virtually unlimited variety of offensive weapons at your command.

But even more importantly, this entire offense is so simple to operate that it could easily be installed on a junior high school level. Conversely, the Area Key Offense is versatile enough to contain the elements of sophistication needed to operate on a high school or college level, without sacrificing this same simplicity.

In fact, one of the primary reasons for writing this book was a series of conversations I had with coaches representing all levels of competition from junior high school to college. In the course of these general "bull sessions" at clinics, summer camps, and casual affairs, I had been asked about the Area Key Offense and its principles of operation. The small portion of information I could transfer in those short conversations was so well-received from coaches at all levels that I decided to share my ideas with a wider audience.

This book makes no exaggerated claims. It doesn't promise anyone a championship. That only comes through extreme dedication and hard, exhausting work on all phases of the game. Nor does it present a rigid system or dogmatic set of principles under which you must operate. My experience has shown that most coaches are suspicious of instant success schemes, and they are equally "turned off" by new offenses which require all-or-nothing commitments.

If one of your weak points is man-for-man offense, however, and if you are a creative and imaginative coach, this book has much to offer. It not only gives a complete description of all of the principles under which the Area Key offense operates, but also recognizes that each coach has his own individual philosophy, personality, and ideas. For this reason, this book has some unique features.

If you are generally satisfied with your present offense, but feel that it has some rough edges, there is a chapter devoted to an explanation of ways in which you may blend the ideas of the Area Key Offense into your present system. If, on the other hand, you choose to adopt the Area Key Offense as your basic form of attack, you will find a chapter which encourages and even stresses the importance of bringing your own imagination into the operation of the offense. If you've had the desire to experiment or "open up," the Area Key Offense can offer you this freedom and opportunity.

This book offers a fresh and unique approach to man-for-man offense. By adding your own ideas, you can maintain this uniqueness while simultaneously building an offense which is really an extension of yourself as a coach.

Most important of all, however, this book presents an offense which has proven itself to be successful with ordinary talent. When extraordinary talent was available, the results were proportionately greater.

Duane Ford

CONTENTS

Countering the Half-Court Trap . . . Attacking Combination Defenses . . . Attacking Traditional Zones . . . Adjusting to Multiple Defenses.

Observations and Recommendations Regarding Zone Offense . . . How to Evaluate a Zone Offense . . . General Zone Offensive Theory . . . How to Use Versatile Post Positions in Attacking Zones . . . How to Use Multiple Formations in a Zone Attack . . . Alignments for Various Zones . . . Free-lancing in the Zone Offense . . . Special Tactics to Create Openings.

THE AREA KEY OFFENSE:

A New Multiple Attack
for Basketball

1 | Advantages of the Area Key Offense

Adopting a new man-for-man offensive system is no small matter. The impetus to do so usually results from one of two basic sources. Either you're a beginning coach who presently has nothing to work with and must make some decision on what offensive strategy to employ, or you're an experienced coach who is dissatisfied in whole or in part with your present system. But, whether you are just "shopping around" for the first time or making an "exchange," you should be aware of exactly what you are looking for before you make your decision. Then, when you find a product (or process) that meets your requirements, you will have something suitable.

The fact that you are reading this book probably indicates that you fall into one of the two categories mentioned above. Assuming, therefore, that you are in the market for a new man-for-man offensive system, I feel it is only fair to outline at the start exactly what principles the Area Key Offense was built upon. I will do so in terms of what advantages I think the Area Key Offense provides. If you know exactly what you are looking for with respect to the advantages you wish your offense to provide, and if the principles of this offense meet your requirements, I sincerely believe this book can be of great value to you.

The first advantage the Area Key Offense provides is a very simple one—it is new, and to a great extent *totally unique in scope and structure*. This, in itself, presents the defense with special problems. Though in theory a sound man-for-man defense is supposed to be able to counter any offensive movements, any of us who have played man-for-man defense know that the offense has the initial advantage in that it knows where it wants to go. Defense is, therefore, a matter of reaction in most cases. This situation can be reversed only if the defense can prevent the offense from doing what it wants to do, and this can only happen if the defense knows beforehand what to expect. Where a traditional offensive system is employed this possibility is much more likely to occur, since most conscientious coaches are well aware of the principles of the more popular offenses whether they use them or not. Much collective effort of defensive-minded coaches also goes into stopping these popular offenses. Any coach who has ever attended a clinic or worked at a basketball camp knows that in the course of general "bull sessions" the question, "How do you stop such-and-such an offense?", is eventually asked.

There are definite advantages, therefore, in employing a new offensive system, since, all things being equal, the uniqueness alone may be enough to initially put you "one up" on the defense.

However, simply being unique never got anyone through an entire game much less a whole season. An offense must offer substantial tangible advantages to prove truly effective.

Obtaining the High-Percentage Shot

The first of these should be some type of designed-in provisions for *consistently obtaining the high-percentage shot*. Any team which continuously takes low-percentage shots won't score much, and an offense which doesn't produce points is useless. Granted, the term high-percentage shot is relative. If you have the great shooter, it may be a 20- to 25-foot bomb. Generally speaking, however, I think most of us coaches think more in terms of the unmolested 10- to 15-foot jumper or lay-up.

Naturally, if you have the good outside shooter, there's nothing to stop you from taking the 20- to 25-foot shot when it presents itself. It's just nice to know you don't have to rely on it by design. Going a step further, if you can make the 25-foot jumper, you can also make the 15-foot shot—probably more often. Why not look for it?

As you will see later in the book, all of our set plays are designed for the 10- to 15-foot jump shot. The standard options are an attempt to get even closer—ultimately, the lay-up.

Realizing Other Advantages

Always taking the good shot is one thing; always making it is quite another. Any sound offense should anticipate the missed shot and thereby be able to provide *adequate rebounding position*. In the Area Key Offense, there should be no less than three rebounders near the basket (one on each side and in front) on set plays, and in most cases they would be the bigger men.

In the event the offensive rebound is not secured, there should then be some arrangement for a *smooth and quick transition from offense to defense*. With the Area Key Offense, there is always a back guard and generally two men on each side of the court.

These principles are nothing new and are common to almost all consistently effective offenses. But there are also some other essential advantages which I feel an offense should provide, and not all currently popular offenses incorporate them into the system.

Providing a Balanced Attack

The first of these is *balance*. Though most coaches seek balance in their offense, the exact meaning of the term varies considerably from coach to coach. To some it means a proper ratio between an inside and outside attack, between the longer jump shot and the lay-up. To others the term is directional or spatial. A balanced attack from this point of view means that both sides of the court are worked equally. Still others feel that a balanced attack should involve several players scoring consistently, rather than relying on just one scorer to carry the bulk of the offensive load.

All of these definitions are valid, and realistically they should all be considered as part of a balanced attack. But I would go one step further, especially in regard to the last viewpoint. Though some coaches feel that two or three scorers can and should take the vast majority of their team's shots, I am firmly convinced that a total team effort in all phases of the game is best served by an offense which *offers every player an equal opportunity to score*. In most cases, those players who are less proficient offensively are well aware of their shortcomings and will not seek to monopolize the offense. When the team is in trouble, they will go to the best offensive player without you asking them. They want to win too. But it is important for their own sense of belonging that they at least have an equal *opportunity* to score as a part of the general offensive design. When the game is well in hand, they will probably take their share of the shots. But in some offenses, they don't even have this chance. If and when you do need them to carry their share of the load, they may be unable to do so either from a lack of self-confidence or experience. For this reason, I believe that a truly balanced attack should be geared to keeping everyone satisfied—even if only potentially.

In the Area Key Offense, one play is designed for guards, another for inside men, and the other two basic plays for a combination of inside and outside men. In all plays there are basic options designed to fit all players. You will naturally come to rely on those plays and options which prove most effective. But the others are there if and when you want them.

Aside from this, there is the matter of substitutions to consider. For example, suppose your ball handling guard is one of your weakest scorers, but his replacement, though deficient in other areas of the game, is an excellent shooter. Does your present offense contain provisions for utilizing the substitute's talents, or is it designed around the first unit? Or perhaps you have special plays designed just for him which the rest of the team must learn for those moments when you can afford to use him? If your offense can't capitalize on his ability, you're losing a great opportunity. If you have to work on a series of special plays, you're wasting valuable team practice time. In any event, the situation could be remedied by having an offense so balanced in opportunity that it could adequately exploit the strengths of *every* team member without necessitating any special adjustments.

Adapting the Offense

If you are in agreement up to this point, you may still be asking yourself a logical question. Suppose I like the offense presented here; will I have difficulty in making the transition to this new offense? Regardless of whether you're a veteran coach or a first-year man, this question is a valid one. Veteran coaches must consider the changeover from previous patterns to new ones, and a new coach still has to work with boys who played before under someone else's system. In either case, there is the problem that old patterns may stay in the mind of the players causing a certain amount of conflict.

When I was considering the development of a new offense, this was one of the problems with which I had to contend. To solve it I first made the assumption that most offenses are *built upon basic fundamental offensive principles,* and, therefore, any new offense would have to *rely* on these same basic maneuvers (give-and-go, picks-and-screens, pick-and-roll, etc.) in order to minimize conflict and achieve a positive transfer of learning. Elaborate patterns calling for complex and unusual maneuvers and responses may look fine on paper, but the difficulties in teaching them to players already grounded in certain basic fundamentals can be enormous.

Psychologists confirm the fact that a positive transfer of learning takes place much more readily when similar responses can be given to new stimuli than vice-versa. In fact a negative transfer is likely to occur if the situation is reversed.

What this means in terms of installing an offense is that learning will occur more readily if the new patterns are compatible with previously learned maneuvers. Since ease of learning is essential to the success of any offense, a new system should provide this compatibility whenever possible.

If your players can already execute the basic offensive maneuvers, you should have little trouble making this transition. If they cannot, it would be wise to skill them in this area before even attempting to implement the Area Key Offense, for these maneuvers are not only the foundation of the offense, but to a large extent they *are* the offense.

Simple to Learn

Learning an offense, however, involves more than the ability to make and perform certain maneuvers in a new context. For the offense to be smoothly executed, the players must fully understand the total system under which they are operating. They must know their own responsibilities and have adequate knowledge of everyone else's responsibilities also, in order that movements can be properly anticipated. In addition, they must be able to read keys and react accordingly. These things can only be accomplished by incorporating another essential advantage into your offense—*simplicity.*

To achieve this, the Area Key Offense has reduced the number of patterns to a manageable level. There are only four standard plays, three of which are highly similar in execution. Also, as you will see, all of the plays follow a definite *sequence* of movements so each can build upon the others rather than occurring in random fashion as is common with many offenses.

However, simplicity can backfire if the defense can capitalize on it. With the Area Key Offense, this should never be the case. In fact, some of the more outstanding advantages of this offense center around its ability to counteract defensive adjustments designed to stop it.

Difficult to Scout

Obviously, before the opposing coach can draw up a game plan, he must first understand the manner in which your offense operates. He usually does this by scouting. Of primary importance in scouting is the matter of detecting keys. This is extremely difficult in the Area Key Offense, for as you will see later, it *operates without any easily detectable keys*.

In terms of systematic operations, frequency is the next important aspect of offensive scouting. Where does the offense begin to attack and where does it go from there? Here the scout can have a field day, for the areas of attack are quite well-defined and constantly pursued. However, this may be of little more value than it is for a general defending a key position to know he will be attacked eventually. The question is: When and how will the attack come? Any attempt to fortify a particular area will only weaken other areas. If it all boils down to a simple guessing game, this *self-adjusting offense* is well-prepared to play it. You will find an entire chapter devoted to countering specific defensive adjustments later in the book.

But, even if your opponent does not have your team well-scouted, a properly drilled team can still make defensive adjustments as a normal response to your movements. Therefore, an offense should contain provisions for *continuity of movement* in case any particular maneuver fails. This offense contains such continuity and should not break down after the first try for the basket simply because of an astute defensive play. It keeps on attacking until a vital mistake is made somewhere.

Also, while on the matter of adjustments, it must be recognized that man-for-man defenses vary considerably in structure in that some offer constant pressure and overplay, while others present a sagging effect. The

Area Key Offense is designed to attack either variety with equal effectiveness without deviating from the normal patterns whatsoever.

Control Game Tempo

This fact is especially important when it comes to the aspect of *controlling game tempo*. The defense may sag or overplay, depending upon the type of tempo it may wish to establish. An offense which must alter its plan of attack because of the structure of the defense lets the defense dictate tempo. This should never be the case. Defense can influence tempo, but the offense should control it!

However, this is only true if the offensive strategy contains provisions for controlling tempo. Some offenses are quick striking, while others are more deliberate. To my way of thinking, an offense should offer both capabilities without any special alterations in patterns. In this way you can speed up or slow down the attack at will, while still putting the same basic pressure on the defense so it cannot feel free to gamble or adjust.

The Area Key Offense can put such pressure on the defense while still controlling the tempo because one of its most striking advantages is the *enormous number of play possibilities* it affords. The four basic plays themselves, which can be run from many formations, not only offer a wide variety of striking capabilities, but many different approaches to scoring as well. If this isn't enough to keep a defense honest, the almost limitless number of options certainly should keep it too preoccupied to worry about adjusting or gambling to influence tempo.

The wide variety of play possibilities also produces many other benefits as well. It *makes general defensive anticipation and adjustment extremely difficult.* It allows you to *take advantage of a particularly poor defender or exploit a structural weakness.* And ultimately, it *permits you to use your own personnel most effectively.*

Very few teams are blessed with an entire squad of "complete" offensive players. Usually we coaches are faced with a situation where most players excel in some areas but are weak in others, while one player may be extremely strong. To devise an offense around the strengths of a particular player may seem sound enough, but if he falters our whole effort can disintegrate. To ignore his strengths and develop an offense which exploits the general talents of the team as a whole may leave us wanting in certain critical situations. Ideally, you should have an offense which accomplishes both purposes. This situation is much more likely to occur if the number and type of scoring possibilities are enlarged. When the players are not versatile, the offense must be.

How you use your substitutes will also affect the ultimate success of your offensive game. One aspect of this was dealt with earlier in the chapter in regard to scoring capabilities. Another dimension of the problem of substitutes centers upon positioning.

This problem became clear to me one year when I had two excellent 6'5" starters, either of which was prone to get in foul trouble on a given night. In a difficult game, I had full confidence in only two substitutes —one 5'7" and the other 5'8".

To replace a 6'5" post man with a 5'7" guard requires a bit of personnel juggling. Thanks to the Area Key Offense, the problem was not that difficult to overcome. We usually went from a one-guard front to a two-guard front and still ran our regular offense. When the situation arose, we could also attack from a double post, single post, or no post at all, depending on our personnel at the time. The important thing is that the alignment did not affect the operation of the regular patterns, and each player could still utilize his special talents when this situation occurred.

Losing an effective offensive player is bad enough. Having to make wholesale revisions in offensive operation because he is on the bench can be disastrous.

Of course, if you have a competent replacement for all, or almost all, positions, you are truly blessed and need not concern yourself about this problem. However, I tend to believe that most coaches are not so fortunate. If you are faced with this difficulty, the multiple formation aspect of this offense alone should be of tremendous value.

Up to this point you may be interested in some of the advantages of the Area Key Offense, but still you may be somewhat skeptical of adopting an entirely new system. Perhaps, then, there is one other element of the offense you may want to consider.

If you have read other books explaining alternative offenses or have attended clinics where such offenses are explained, you may have been "scared away" by the toal commitments required in most cases. The Area Key Offense requires no such total commitments. What's offered here is a basic format. All of the advantages listed thus far are present in this offense if you choose to adopt it as your basic offense. Many of these same advantages can be obtained through a partial adoption as well. It is simple enough to learn that it can be easily implemented as an alternate offense. It is also versatile enough that it can be blended into or used as an extension of another offense. In essence, it is the type of offense that you can experiment with enough to determine whether it is applicable for your circumstances without necessitating the type of total commitment you may be unwilling to make. It's not the type of offense you'll be forced to "live or die with." More will be said about this in the chapter devoted to blending area keys into your present offense.

Give it a *fair chance*, and I'm quite sure it will prove its value.

There is one final advantage of this offense I would like you to consider. Whether you are a junior high, high school, or college coach, you should find this offense applicable. You will find few offenses as simplistic and yet so sophisticated as the Area Key Offense.

If you do look upon coaching as a profession, you probably have ambitions of progressing as far as your talents can carry you. Each time you make a "move up," you don't want to be forced to adopt a new system of operation more consistent with your new level of coaching. What you ultimately want is an offense which can grow with you. The Area Key Offense offers you this opportunity.

As the type of player you coach increases in ability, your offense can increase in effectiveness. As you move up, you will have the freedom to explore new possibilities, yet all within a familar framework. Rather than being forced to choose among alternatives, you will be free to apply virtually all of the maneuvers you learned along the way.

How many other offenses can say the same?

Above all else, however, the ultimate factor that must be considered in evaluating an offense is a very simple one. Does it really work in competition?

Many offenses "sound" good when they're described, and they may look excellent on a blackboard. But playing "x and o" in a locker room is not the same as performing on the court.

Though statistics can be manipulated to mean whatever you want them to mean, they at least afford some index of a team's performance. So, perhaps the following statistics can help clarify the question of whether or not the Area Key Offense really works.

Over a seven-year period, our school's record was 24 wins and 128 losses. Since the Area Key Offense has been installed, this same school, against the same competition, has averaged 18-plus wins per year (72%). During this time, our offensive output has increased by an average of 12 points per game. Of course, this in itself is nothing spectacular. But the 12-point increase does not tell the whole story. Because of the ease in improving our offensive game, we found time to stress defense more heavily. Subsequently, our defensive average had dropped more than 13 points. That's a total improvement of 25 points per game. Also, we rarely fast break and have seldom had the type of players who can gain a lot of easy baskets through utilization of the press. Almost all of our baskets result from the regular patterns of our offense. This is not because our offense is incompatible with a pressing and fast-break type of game. As you will see in a later chapter, it can complement this type of game very well. Generally, we just haven't had the personnel who were suited to this style of play.

Granted, the vast improvement could be attributed in some part to a change of system, better personnel, a better feeder program, etc.—but I sincerely feel a large part of our total success is due to the Area Key Offense.

For one thing, our increased emphasis on defense could not have been possible without having an offense which was effective yet simple enough to be perfected without spending an inordinate amount of time developing it. If you also stress a strong defensive effort, I'm sure you'll find this offense makes an excellent companion to your defensive game.

There is one other statistic you may wish to consider in evaluating the actual effectiveness of the Area Key Offense. Every year we find fewer and fewer teams willing to play us man-for-man as a basic defense. Most of those that do are primarily man-for-man ball clubs anyway. Very few teams who employ multiple defenses feel a man-for-man defense is the best way to stop us. In fact, it has come to the point where we often try to force our opponents to abandon a zone as a normal part of our game plan by holding the ball near mid-court once we have the lead. But even then we are more likely to find a team attempting zone traps or "committing suicide" by spreading out to cover us. Then, of course, we'll take what they give us.

Whereas our players used to dread playing against a man-for-man defense, they now express the desire to see one. Perhaps this more than any statistic indicates the effectiveness of the Area Key Offense.

Now, briefly, I will summarize the advantages of the Area Key Offense which have evidenced themselves for us.

Uniqueness of approach

Consistent access to the high-percentage shot

Adequate rebounding position

Smooth transition to defense

Total balance in attack

Equal opportunity for all to score

Ability to exploit total personnel strengths

Reliance on basic offensive maneuvers

Ease of learning and execution (simplicity)

Elimination of detectable keys

Continuity of movement and sequence of patterns

Flexibility for self-adjustment to defensive variations

Control of game tempo

Enormous number of play possibilities

2 | *Keying Your Offense by Areas*

$\mathbf{R}$egardless of the type of offense you have used or considered up to now, you must certainly be aware of the fact that every offense must be keyed in some way. Players must be able to anticipate their own movements and those of teammates as well, if the offense is to run smoothly and effectively. Keys accomplish this purpose.

Even a free-lance offense is geared to operate on the assumption that players can read the movements of teammates and react accordingly. When a pick is set, a roll can usually be expected. Of course, a great deal of experience and fundamental knowledge of the game is necessary to effectively operate a total free-lance system. Players must also play together extensively before they can accurately "read" each other's movements. Most high schools, and even many colleges, often cannot meet these requirements and instead must rely on a more direct and precise way to key their offenses.

Traditional Methods of Keying an Offense and Their Disadvantages

Certainly, when it comes to keying an offense, football teams are one up on us. They have the advantage of the privacy of a huddle. No way has yet been found to achieve the equivalent of the huddle for basketball.

However, it is often found that a play called in the huddle will not work because of certain defensive adjustments. Then the quarterback is forced to operate on the same terms our guards constantly do in basketball. A technique long used in basketball is the only alternate—the audible.

These audibles, or verbal keys, have had a very prominent place in basketball for years, and they are quite simple to utilize. The key man will simply shout out a number, color, name, or other designated signal to start a play. However, this system is not as easy as it appears on the surface. Unlike the football quarterback, the basketball player cannot ask the referee to quiet the crowd. With more and more gyms being filled to capacity, crowds are often quite boisterous. In the heat of a close contest, the noise can be so unbearable that such verbal keys simply cannot be heard by all of the players, especially in today's larger gyms. If only one player fails to hear the key, it can disrupt the entire pattern.

But such keys also present more general difficulties. For one thing, if the offense can be expected to pick them up, it must stand to reason that the opponents can also intercept them. Of course, interpreting such keys is another matter entirely. However, it must be understood that the more complex these keys become in order to fool the defense, the more difficult it is for the offensive team to interpret them. This same principle is true in reverse.

If you use only a few basic verbal signals to key your offense, an astute defense should eventually understand their meaning. Conversely, if you have a rather large number of complex keys, you may easily find some members of your team as confused as the opponents. I wish I had a dollar for every player who stood perfectly still mentally computing his assignment when he was supposed to be setting a pick or making a cut 20 feet away from his chosen spot of contemplation. Don't waste a time-out finding out what happened either. He always seems to remember his assignment somewhere between mid-court and the sideline. Then you get that familiar nod of the head before you say a word.

To overcome these difficulties of the verbal keys, many coaches have chosen an alternative method—hand signals. With this method, the ballhandler may raise any number of fingers or a closed or open hand to indicate the particular pattern desired. Often the finger signals and the fist are used in combination.

Though such hand signals overcome some of the difficulties of verbal keys, they often raise their own particular set of problems.

Confusion can occur when one player or another is trying to establish position and is not looking when the signal is flashed. It is also possible that a player may be shielded from seeing the signal. This problem can be partially solved by having the hand raised in a deliberate fashion for an adequate period of time. However, with more and more teams employing full-court pressure defenses, the man who keys the offense may not even have the ball. If he does, he usually has all he can do just to bring the ball up court. With a defender hounding him, it's pretty difficult to find the time or a free hand to give a clear and deliberate signal. Constant harassment of the ballhandler alone can easily create havoc with an offense geared to hand signals.

In any event, whether verbal or hand signals are used, any coach who patiently scouts an opponent will no doubt have some idea of what the various signals mean, and he can appraise his players on what to expect when certain plays are called.

Even when an opponent is not adequately scouted though, the defense still has the alternative of on-the-spot adjustments. When playing defense, our players are instructed to listen or watch for detectable keys. When they detect one, they are told to concentrate on what their men do on that signal. The next time they detect that same key, they should try to prevent their men from making that same move again. This goes for everyone.

For instance, if a point guard were to call out "number one" and then hit the left wing and set a pick opposite the ball, our man defensing the point guard should make a mental note of what his man did on the "number one" play. The next time he hears the same play called, he should react accordingly. First, he should try to prevent the pass to the wing, and if unsuccessful, force his man to move away from his normal path. Everyone else should do likewise. This may not stop a particular play, but it should interfere with the timing. This may be enough to disrupt a team's offensive effectiveness.

Minimal Key Offenses

Recognizing that these difficulties are inherent in the traditional methods of keying an offense, but not willing to adopt a total free-lance system, many coaches have gone to a continuity type of offense. With a continuity offense, no particular set plays are called. Rather, the entire team is involved in a series of specified movements or patterns designed to take advantage of defensive weaknesses or mistakes. The keys are built into the pattern itself, since each player's movements in the total pattern are designated beforehand.

The difficulty here is that scoring opportunities must be recognized when they occur and taken advantage of immediately. Unlike the set play offenses, the offensive team cannot anticipate such openings. They often come unexpectedly and many times go unnoticed. Conversely, scoring opportunities are sometimes diagnosed incorrectly. Players see openings that aren't really there.

Continuity offenses are also easy to scout. Though they rely mostly on fundamental maneuvers (picks, screens, rolls, and basic cuts) and can be very effective in exploiting weaknesses, the scouting report tells almost exactly what to expect, and defensive preparations can easily be made, at least on paper. If the expected pattern is adjusted to, the offense can be stopped or severely hampered. There is little element of surprise. It simply resolves itself into a battle between the execution of basic offensive and defensive techniques.

Though this is ultimately the determiner of the outcome of most contests, it need not always be so. The offense still has the advantage of making the first move, and the element of surprise should never be underestimated.

Keying by Area

Probably the ideal offense would combine the best aspects of the existing systems. It would offer the definite security and design of the set play offense; the ability of the free-lance offense to strike unexpectedly; and the constant pressure of attack from the continuity offense.

The major problem in developing such an offense, of course, is the same old item of how to key it. I realized that if I could find some way to key such a comprehensive offense, we would have a truly unique offensive advantage.

The solution came through the simple process of extending a basic play we had used quite effectively in the past. Though this one play was quite useful when run to completion, we often found that certain option maneuvers could be used in conjunction with it. Thus we had the beginnings of using two of the three basic types of offenses—the set play and the free-lance offenses. All we had to do to achieve continuity was to trace the movements of the play (if run to completion) and see how we could revert back to these movements if any intervening options failed.

As you will see when the basic play is explained in the next chapter, the ball moves in and out of several designated areas on the court. Since the ball was usually in or very near one of these basic areas at all times, we found on experimentation that it was not difficult to complete our play from whatever spot a particular option maneuver failed.

Essentially, then, what we were really doing was keying our offense by areas on the court. We had no use for hand or verbal signals, and we didn't have to live or die with the players' ability to correctly diagnose a free-lance opportunity.

With the premise of area keys in mind, the development of a total offensive system was simply a matter of expansion of play possibilities and general refinement.

Basically, here is how the area keys operate. As shown in Diagram 2-1, the court is divided into a series of seven designated areas—three on each side of the basket and one at the top of the foul circle. Both sides of the court are numbered the same so that all situations are identical, regardless of the side on which the plays begin or continue. In this way, the number of plays and options are doubled.

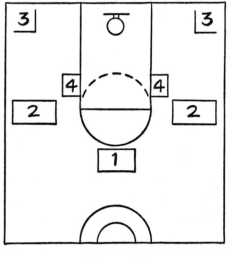

Diagram 2-1

Area 1 begins just above the top of the foul circle. It is as wide as the foul lane and extends about 8 to 10 feet back toward the mid-court circle. This area is most commonly referred to as the "point."

Area 2 comprises what is generally known as the "wings." If the foul line were to be extended to the sideline, it would split the area in half. It should begin about 5 feet from the foul lane and extend to a point about 5 feet from the sideline. It should also extend about 3 feet on each side of the foul-line extended.

Area 3 is an approximate 4- or 5-foot square located near the intersection of the sideline and end line. In fact, if you have 3-foot restraining lines bordering your court, the intersection of these lines would form an ideal outer boundary for Area 3.

Area 4 is the smallest area, and it is the most definitely defined area as well. Since the basic play is completed at this point, it must be fairly precise. The outer edge of the line marking the foul lane forms the inside boundary. This area should extend only about 2 feet toward the sideline. Vertically, the area is also only about 2 feet long. Ideally, the second line from the foul line marking the rebounding spaces on the lane would form the exact spot to which we would want to move the ball, but we allow a foot on either side of this line for latitude. Extending this area farther from the basket will give us a longer shot than we want. This will become clearer when the Drop-Step Play is explained.

Defining these areas so explicitly may seem restrictive. In actuality, though, we do allow some degree of latitude. If a player approaches the general vicinity, we will continue the play from that point. We are only adamant about Area 4 being virtually intact.

The reasons for defining the area as we do are quite simple. First of all, we want our players to receive the ball at all times in a spot where they represent a positive offensive threat. In this way, our opponents must play us honest. This not only spreads the defense and opens up the middle, but it also allows us to utilize our basic 1-on-1 maneuvers. If we move to the areas as defined, our players are almost always within the 15- to 20-foot shooting range. We feel we can usually shoot our percentage from this range though we like to go closer. Why jeopardize your chances for a better shot by constantly receiving the ball out of shooting range? If you have to put the ball on the floor to represent any kind of threat, you're eliminating much of your individual maneuvering while putting constant pressure on the ball handling phase of your game.

Secondly, the areas as outlined are close enough together that most of our passes are quite short. In general, the shorter the passes the more accurate they should be. Cut down the distance and you cut down the margin for error.

Thirdly, and conversely, the areas are also far enough apart that "crowding" is prevented. No defender can simultaneously watch two offensive men. Likewise, any attempt at a double team leaves us with enough time and room to react in a positive manner.

We feel that the spacing of our areas offers us the maximum balance between a shortening of passing lanes and the prevention of overcrowding.

Next, we should consider the matter of numbering the areas in se-

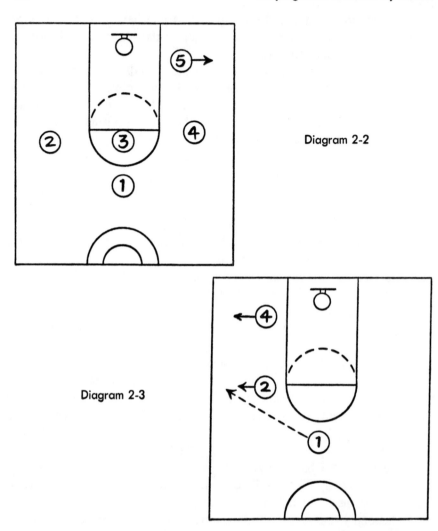

Diagram 2-2

Diagram 2-3

quence. This is not done for convenience; it is essential to the operation of the offense.

Since there are no verbal or hand signals, this offense is based upon the movement of the ball in or out of a series of potentially live areas. Whenever the ball is advanced into any one of these areas, the next area in sequence would become "live." An area becoming live simply means that the nearest man moves to that area, prepared to receive the ball, *regardless of who it is.* The one exception to this rule is that the ball is usually (though not always) advanced from Area 3 to Area 4 on a dribble.

This process would continue until the ball is advanced to Area 4 where the basic play is completed. If no shot is available at that point, the ball is simply moved to another area and movement begins again.

For example, in Diagram 2-2 we are aligned in a 1-3-1 formation.

The ball is originally in Area 1, so Area 2 is live. Since there is already a man there in normal position, no adjustments are necessary. O_4 would simply receive the pass. There is no one in Area 3, however. Therefore, it is necessary for O_5, the nearest man, to advance to that area.

From a tight 1-2-2 set (Diagram 2-3) though, both O_2 and O_4 would have to move to "live" Areas 2 and 3, since neither of them occupied these areas when they became live.

For flexibility's sake, there are some slight variations from these basic rules. If no one is occupying an area and the man with the ball still retains his dribble, it is often advantageous to allow him the option of dribbling the ball into an area as is usually done from Area 3 to 4. You may also experience occasions when it is useful or necessary to completely by-pass an area. This presents no difficulty since, whenever an area is by-passed, the next area from the ball still becomes live. Both of these situations most often occur in regard to Areas 1 and 2 and especially with a 2-1-2 formation.

As shown in Diagram 2-4, because of the 2-1-2 formation, the ball does not usually enter Area 1; hence, it is completely by-passed. Also, since O_1 has retained his dribble, he simply advances the ball to Area 2 with the dribble. Once the ball has entered Area 2, Area 3 becomes live and O_5 moves to that position. From here the play can be run quite normally.

At this point another important rule should be noted. As was mentioned earlier, the ball is usually advanced to Area 4 on the dribble. There are occasions, however, when the ball enters Area 4 through passing. In fact, there are two plays specifically designed to capitalize on this situation when it occurs.

Diagram 2-4

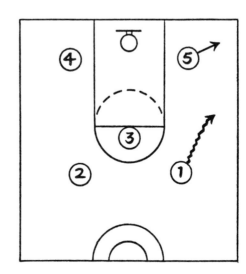

Nevertheless, once the ball has entered Area 3, caution should be exercised in entering Area 4 for a pass. First of all, that area is usually reserved for our base-line men or pivot men, and whenever the ball is in Area 3, Area 4 should be entered only when a definite scoring opportunity is anticipated. If a pass is not received, the area is cleared quickly to make room for the man coming from Area 3.

This rule does not apply when the ball is in either of the other two areas. For example, if the ball is in Area 2, you may freely flash a man into the pivot from the weak side. If he doesn't get the ball, he may hold there for a possible pass from Area 3. Then the above rule would apply.

If the man in Area 4 is open and receives the pass, he may try to score, or he may simply hold the ball there for the completion of one of our plays.

In any event, the important point to remember is this: Whatever movements occur, the ball will always be in or near one of the key areas. For continuity the ball can merely be advanced to the next area, either through passing or dribbling.

Advantages of Using Area Keys

Since all but one of our four plays are designed to be completed in Area 4, an almost infinite variety of offensive maneuvers can be executed before reaching that area without curtailing the essential patterns of the offense. Regardless of how often option maneuvers break down in the meantime, the plays can still be executed without readjusting.

Though we have four basic plays that this offense revolves around, I can rarely think of an occasion when we have run any of the plays to completion more than ten times on any given night. By far the greatest majority of our points come from options which break us free before the completion of a play.

Also, you will very seldom find our players standing around after an option fails to yield a shot. There is almost no break in the action. The ball is simply moved to another area, and we continue on looking for other opportunities elsewhere.

Such freedom and spontaneity makes defensive adjustments very difficult. Even when the defense knows your basic pattern, they must rely on you to follow it mechanically. If they overplay to stop the movement into a particular area, they are vulnerable somewhere else. In fact, this is the reason most of our scores come before the completion of a play. After a few early baskets off the plays, most teams are so intent on interrupting our basic patterns that they weaken themselves in a total sense. Of course if they let us run our regular patterns, we would continue to score anyway. They really don't have much choice.

Since the basic content of this chapter deals with keying on offense, there is one other way in which you can confuse your opponents. Because of the eagerness of most scouts and some defensive players to look for noticeable keys, you may find it to your advantage on occasion to give them a series of false keys. This can be done very easily. Periodically, when your ballhandler comes down court, have him call out a number or name, or give some kind of hand signal. If your opponents make note of the movements which follow that particular ''key,'' they will no doubt be somewhat befuddled when that same ''key'' given again elicits a totally different response. They should be equally confused when those same movements follow an entirely different ''key.''

It must be recognized that a worthy opponent will eventually catch on to your deception. Even so, they still will have wasted some valuable time and energy in trying to analyze your strategy. That in itself may be worth your while to try false keys. It may also eventually discourage an opponent from trying to do so in the future.

Obviously, though, you must be prepared to face the reality that some opponents will eventually be able to make the necessary adjustments to seriously impair your offense. After all, when a group of well-coached, experienced players play the same man in the same position for half a ball game or more, they are bound to correctly anticipate certain movements. To give a team more moves than even the best defense can handle is a coach's dream. More often than not though, most offenses can't handle such extreme variety. Either they become so confused that they do little or nothing in terms of movement, or they come to rely on a few basic maneuvers which have worked well in the past. When I mentioned earlier that the Area Key Offense offers an almost infinite variety of scoring possibilities, I did not mean that every team could employ this infinite variety of maneuvers. The variety is there for all teams, but not all teams can handle it. We have used all of the options described in this book—but not in any given year. They have resulted from cumulative experience. Like our own teams from year to year, I'm sure your teams will find a certain limited number of options to their liking and they will perfect them.

But still, what do you do when a team begins to stop your favorite maneuvers as a game progresses simply because each defender is zeroing in on his man's basic moves? We have found a rather simple solution to this problem which is a direct result of using area keys. Since the offense depends upon the movement of the *ball* in or out of the designated key areas, the original alignment of players is of little consequence in operating the offense. Hence, one of the most striking elements of the total offense becomes possible; i.e., the use of multiple formations.

If a particular defender playing a wing man comes to know his man too well (diagnoses his movements accurately), it is quite easy to take this man from the wing and move him to a low post, high post, or guard position, depending on his talent and ability. Now the defender is forced to "see" his man in a new perspective. If the defender found he could stop his man with an overplay for denial on the wing, can he risk this same procedure when his man assumes a guard position? Or if a defensive man found that he could successfully stop a low post man by playing above him, will this same tactic work when his man moves to a high post?

By simply changing the position of men on the court or altering the angle of attack, you add an entirely new dimension to your offense. Teams who can stop your 1-2-2 attack may not be so successful when you strike with a 2-1-2 and roll your post man.

Though your number of options may not be infinite, the angle from which you can execute these options may be so varied that your opponents may think you are executing more maneuvers than you really are.

You may alter your formations after you feel an opponent begins to seriously cramp your style, or you may do so regularly throughout a contest before they get a chance to do so. This is a matter of choice and philosophy, depending upon the psychological state you wish to create in your opponents' minds.

In any event, regardless of the formation you are in, the basic plays remain the same, and your players should be able to execute them with equal efficiency.

More will be said later about how to play multiple formation basketball. A separate chapter is devoted to this phase of the Area Key Offense. To really explain how the total offense operates, however, it is first necessary to elaborate upon the basic plays around which the offense revolves.

3 | *The Drop-Step Play and Basic Team Options*

How to Run the Drop-Step Play

If the Area Key Offense owes its existence to any one thing, it's the Drop-Step Play explained in this chapter.

Though I don't want to get bogged down in a history of the play itself, I do feel obligated to mention that I did not originate it. It was borrowed by way of an assistant coach from Dutch Birch of Lycoming College, who has successfully used the play for several years.

This play in itself is a potent offensive weapon, but no one play can sustain an entire offense. The latitude for contingent options this play allows and the simple sequence of movements involved in its completion are what really made us decide to use it as the foundation of an entire strategy. Though you could probably use the format of many other plays to develop your own system of area keys, I feel this particular play affords the best opportunity to incorporate the advantages of a man-for-man offense explained in the first chapter.

For simplicity, I will explain the Drop-Step Play in its entirety from a 1-2-2 formation as it was originally designed. (In a later chapter, I will

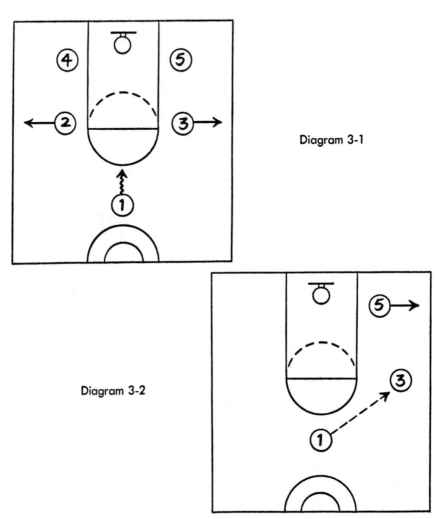

Diagram 3-1

Diagram 3-2

explain how this play can be executed from various other formations as well.) Also, since movements are identical to both sides of the court, the play will be diagramed from the right side only.

As shown in Diagram 3-1, the play is initiated when the ball enters Area 1. Though you may spread your forwards originally in a 1-2-2 formation, we have found that it is better to begin from a tight alignment and "bust out" to Area 2 once the ball enters Area 1. Since many teams try to overplay the wings to deny the pass there, a tight alignment forces the defender inside originally, away from Area 2.

As soon as O_3 breaks free in Area 2, O_1 hits him with a chest pass and holds at the top of the key. When O_3 receives the pass from O_1, O_5 breaks quickly to Area 3, anticipating the pass. Of course, if the man guarding O_3 sags inside, or, if in an attempt to overplay the pass, he overruns the ball, O_3 would have the option of going for an immediate score. If neither of these options presents itself, O_3 would pass to O_5 in Area 3 and the play would continue as shown in Diagram 3-3.

Once O_5 has the ball several things could happen before the ball is advanced to Area 4. In Diagram 3-3 you will notice that after passing to O_5, O_3 cuts to the basket. You will also notice that the cut can take either of two forms. If the defender on O_3 tries to stay between his man and the ball, O_3 will move toward the ball and then execute a backdoor cut. If the defender stands or backs up after the pass, O_3 will move away from the ball and then cut between his man and the ball for what we call a middle or inside cut. Both of these moves are built into the play and are not to be considered extraneous options. If O_3 is open, O_5 should make every effort to get him the ball. In most cases if O_3 is open enough to receive a pass, he should be open enough to score. When O_3 does not get a return pass, he continues on through the lane to the opposite wing.

If O_3 is not open for a return pass, O_5 now has two specific planned options before he advances the ball to Area 4. First he looks for a base-line drive to the basket. This can often occur if his man has tried to overplay the original pass and ended up above or beyond O_5. If his man is playing him head-up after the reception, he may try to fake him out of position for a base-line drive, since he has a complete clear-out situation on his side which gives him free reign for 1-on-1 moves. If he cannot get the drive but has an open 15-foot shot, in most cases (depending upon his ability), he will be encouraged to take this next option.

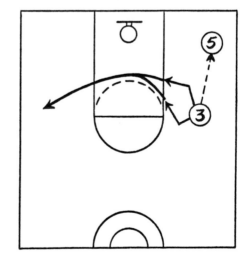

Diagram 3-3

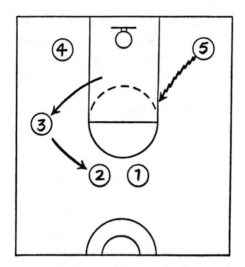

Diagram 3-4

Once he has decided that the return pass to O_3, the base-line drive, or the shot are not feasible, he will simply carry out the next phase of the play. As shown in Diagram 3-4, O_5 advances the ball on the dribble to Area 4 where he awaits the completion of the play. You will also notice in Diagram 3-4 that O_2 has moved to the top of the foul circle to join O_1 in what we call "the marriage." O_2 makes this move as soon as O_3 has made his cut through the lane and into the area occupied by O_2.

When O_5 reaches Area 4 with the ball, O_1 and O_2 move down the foul lane together about 1 to 2 feet apart (Diagram 3-5). This spacing is important since we don't want a defender slipping through a pick we set as we go down the lane. O_1 must also be within arm's length of O_2 to set up the second option which will be discussed shortly.

As the pair at the top of the foul circle proceed down the foul lane together, there are two planned options. The first of these is illustrated in Diagram 3-6. As soon as O_1 and O_2 reach a point just below the ball, O_1 makes a drop-step maneuver and comes back around O_5 for the ball and a quick jump shot behind O_5's screen or the drive. The exact manner in which the drop-step move is executed will be fully explained in the next chapter. It is enough for now to note that on the exchange, O_1 should be able to shoot almost immediately upon receiving the ball. No dribble should be necessary in order to establish the proper footwork for the shot. If a dribble is needed, it will eliminate the fake and consequent drive.

The second option involves a double screen as shown in Diagram 3-7. As O_1 and O_2 begin the move down the lane together, the inside man (nearest the ball) slaps his partner on the back. This is the signal for the outside man (O_2) to complete the drop step.

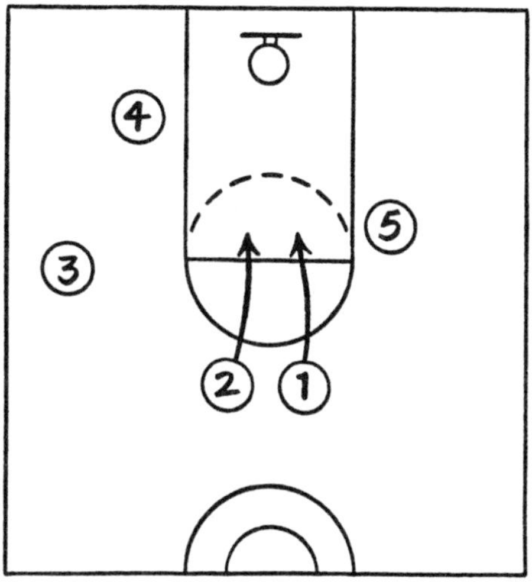

Diagram 3-5

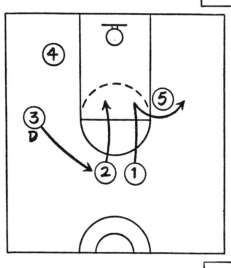

Diagram 3-6

Diagram 3-7

On this option, O_1 stops even with the ball while O_2 goes a step below the ball. O_2 will then come back, hopefully rubbing his man off on O_1, and continues around O_5 for the short hand-off and the jump shot or drive.

It should be pointed out that the inside man is always the one who "calls" this play. It is up to him to decide whether he or his partner will complete the drop step. This rule applies no matter who is at the top of the foul circle, for it will not always be O_1. In the event the second option is called for, it is imperative that the inside man slap the outside man emphatically so there is no doubt as to who completes the play. When we first started to run this option, we found on occasion that no one completed the play, since the outside man was not sure whether he was given the signal or not. If he does not receive an emphatic slap on the back, he must always assume that the inside man will complete the play.

You will note in both Diagrams 3-8 and 3-9 that the man not making the drop-step move continues on down the lane and then sets up a pick for the base-line man opposite the ball. This pick serves a dual purpose, and it is the final portion of the play.

If the man completing the drop step in Diagram 3-6 cannot take the shot, O_4 may be set free by the pick for an easy lay-up or could continue on across the lane for a short base-line jump shot. When O_1 does take the shot, then O_4 is in a better position to rebound. If his man does not switch, a properly set pick would free him entirely for the rebound; whereas, a switch would still create a mismatch, since, in most cases, the man watching O_1 will be a smaller guard. O_1 would also have inside position as a result of a switch. This may help counter his height disadvantage. Without the pick you would have neither inside position nor the mismatch. Therefore, this move is quite important and should not be neglected as a part of the play.

You will notice also in these diagrams that after "the marriage" forms at the top of the circle and both men move down the lane, O_3 proceeds to Area 1. He should arrive there just as the drop-step move is made. This movement also serves two purposes.

If the play falters and no open shot is available, O_3 can receive the pass and start a new play right from that spot. Since the ball is in Area 1, there would be movement to Area 2 immediately, and no adjustments would be necessary (Diagram 3-10).

Also, the position of O_3 at the top of the circle re-establishes balance, both offensively and defensively. The defensive balance is especially important, for if the shot is missed and the opponent grabs the rebound,

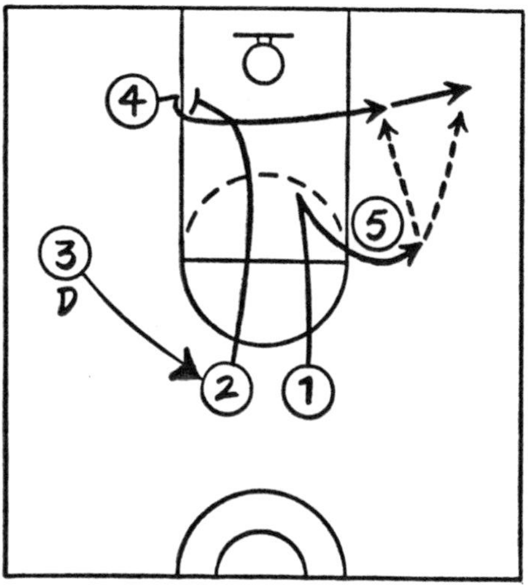

Diagram 3-8

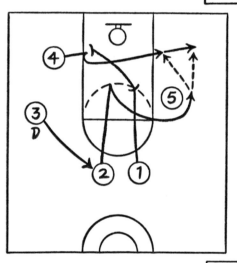

Diagram 3-9

Diagram 3-10

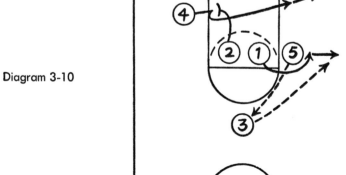

you are in good position to prevent the fast break. Regardless of who the man is in this position, he serves the purpose of a back guard. It is essential to impress this fact upon your players. Since the use of multiple formations may put a forward, or on rare occasions even a base-line man, in this position, he must resist the normal urge to go for the rebound. In these and other diagrams, "D" denotes defensive responsibility.

Since the explanations attached to each of the various movements may have interrupted a sense of the total continuity of the Drop-Step Play, I will now briefly review the movements involved, using the same diagrams.

As shown in Diagram 3-1, as soon as the ball has entered Area 1, Area 2 becomes live, and O_2 and O_3 move to this area on each side of the court. In Diagram 3-2, O_3 receives the pass in Area 2 and then O_5 moves to the next live area—Area 3. After passing the ball to O_5 (Diagram 3-3), O_3 cuts toward the basket. When he does not receive a return pass from O_5, he continues on to Area 2 on the other side of the court. Meanwhile, O_2 and O_1 are forming "the marriage" at the top of the foul circle as O_5 prepares to move out of Area 3 toward Area 4 (Diagram 3-4). Just as O_5 approaches Area 4, O_1 and O_2 start down the lane together (Diagram 3-5) preparing for the drop step. If O_1 does not give O_2 a pat on the back, O_1 completes the drop-step move (Diagram 3-6), and O_2 continues down the lane and sets a pick for O_4 (Diagram 3-8). If O_1 does give the signal to O_2, then O_2 completes the drop step as shown in Diagram 3-7. O_1 then picks for O_4 (Diagram 3-9). As O_1 and O_2 move down the lane, O_3 goes to establish his position in Area 1.

This is how this play would operate if it were run to its completion. However, in many, if not most, instances, opportunities to score arise before the drop-step move is ever made. If the planned options don't create a scoring opportunity, any number of possible free-lance options might. (These free-lance options will be discussed at length in a separate chapter.) Still, the Drop-Step Play affords a certain sense of security. Though it's a potent play in itself, it can also function as a "safety valve" in the Area Key Offense, thereby encouraging a great deal of experimentation which might not otherwise be risked.

Nevertheless, though the Drop-Step Play is the foundation of the Area Key Offense, we found it to our advantage to add a few alternate plays to the offense. There are only three others, and with one exception they really aren't separate plays at all. Two of them are really variations of the drop-step maneuver, the difference being that the drop-step is executed from different angles on the court.

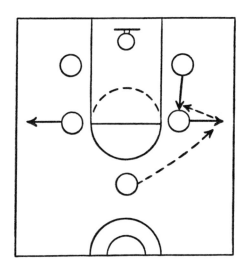

Diagram 3-11

The Scissors

The first of these, the Scissors, was installed as a counter-adjustment to defensive moves designed to keep the man in Area 3 from advancing the ball to Area 4. This was originally the most common ploy used by our opponents who had scouted us extensively. Though certain individual options could usually counter this adjustment, we felt we might not always have the personnel who could successfully execute these options. Therefore, we decided to make a systematic counter-adjustment and leave nothing to chance.

Essentially, the Scissors is an area by-pass play. Rather than have the ball advance on the dribble from Area 3 to Area 4, it is advanced directly to Area 4 from Area 2 with a pass. The play is keyed in a very simple manner. Whenever the man who would normally move to Area 3 (when the ball is in Area 2) positions himself in Area 4, it is a signal to by-pass Area 3.

This situation could occur in either of two ways. As shown in Diagram 3-11, the base-line man in the 1-2-2 formation could move up into Area 4 from another position. Or, as shown in Diagram 3-12, the top man in a stack formation could simply hold his position in Area 4.

Once the man in Area 4 receives the pass, the play is ready for quick execution. The Scissors is so named because it involves a double drop step with the two men crossing paths.

In Diagram 3-13 it is assumed that O_3 has already hit O_5 with the pass. As soon as the pass is received, O_3 executes the drop step from the

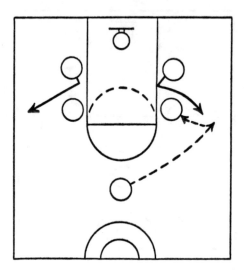

Diagram 3-12

Diagram 3-13

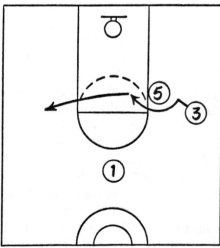

side. If he does not receive the return pass from O_5, he continues across the lane to Area 2 on the other side. As soon as O_3 has completed his drop step (and did not receive the ball), O_1 then executes the drop step from the top of the key—alone (Diagram 3-14). If he does not receive the pass either, he circles back to Area 2 on the ball side.

As with the first play described, the drop-step move is executed in the same manner. The cutter goes slightly below the ball and then comes back around close to the man with the ball, hoping to rub off his defender.

Also, as with the Drop-Step Play, there is continuity if these moves fail to yield a scoring opportunity. The ball can be passed to O_2, who moves to the top of the key as O_1 makes his move. O_2 would then hit Area

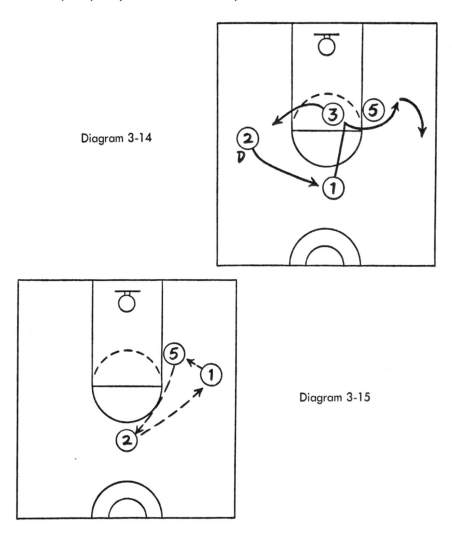

Diagram 3-14

Diagram 3-15

2 on either side and the Scissors could be run again (Diagram 3-15). Of course, the Drop-Step Play could also be run in this situation.

The Side-Drop Play

The third play grew out of an attempt to capitalize more fully on one of our most effective free-lance options—the flash post cut to the ball by a weakside base-line man. Usually if the man making this cut has good inside moves, he frees himself for a high-percentage shot. However, on occasion this move yields no positive results. In such instances, the post man could just throw an outlet pass elsewhere, and we could run the

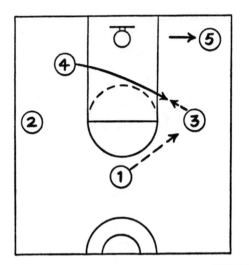

Diagram 3-16

Diagram 3-17

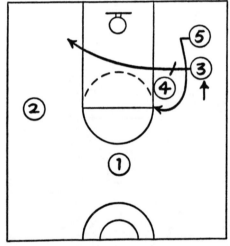

Drop-Step Play. However, we felt that there was a chance to add a new dimension to the offense.

Though the Side Drop is usually run after a flash post cut has been made, there are other instances where a similar situation prevails. Therefore, the play is keyed in this manner: whenever the ball is in Area 4 while both Areas 2 and 3 are occupied to the side of the ball, the Side-Drop Play will be run.

As shown in Diagram 3-16, O_4 flashes into the post (Area 4) when O_3 has the ball and receives the pass. Since O_5 moved to Area 3 after O_3 received the pass, both Areas 2 and 3 are occupied while the ball is in Area 4. If O_4 does not free himself for a score, he keeps the ball there. O_3

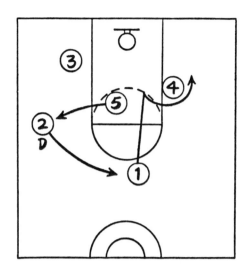

Diagram 3-18

and O_5 then come together for a marriage on the side of the court (Diagram 3-17). Once they are paired, they execute the drop-step move in the same manner as if they were at the top of the foul circle. Though either man can make the drop step, it is usually most effective if the lower man makes the move. The man not making the cut for the ball goes through the lane and establishes rebounding position on the other side of the basket.

If the play cannot be completed, the ball can easily be passed to the man in Area 1 and another play can then begin. Or the play can be extended even further, with the drop step being made from the top of the key also (Diagram 3-18).

The Bounce Pass Play

The last set play in the Area Key Offense is the only one of the four that does not seek to set up a drop-step maneuver as its primary objective. It is the fastest striking play in the offense and one of the most effective if properly executed. Its success is derived primarily from the fact that it begins in *almost* exactly the same manner as all the others except for one small variation. There is, therefore, an element of surprise involved.

The Bounce Pass Play is so named because it is the bounce pass which keys it. In all of the other plays, the ball is advanced to Area 2 with a chest pass. Whenever a bounce pass is made, it is a signal to depart from the usual format.

In Diagram 3-19, O_1 hits O_3 with the bounce pass, and O_5 clears to the corner as usual. However, as soon as the pass is delivered, the man in

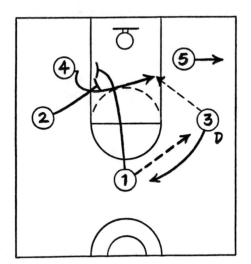

Diagram 3-19

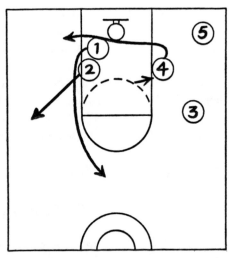

Diagram 3-20

Area 1 (O_1) and the man in Area 2 opposite the ball (O_2) move toward the base line together to set a double pick for O_4. O_4 then goes over the top of the pick and into the foul lane.

Ideally, O_4 should shed his man on the double pick and be open for an easy short jumper or driving lay-up. However, you must be prepared for the possibility that neither of these outcomes will materialize. In fact, you may not even be able to get the ball to O_4.

In this latter event, there should be no confusion as very little adjustment is necessary in order to complete the Drop-Step Play. If O_4 does not get the ball as expected, he simply rolls on through the lane and back to his original position (Diagram 3-20). O_1 and O_2 would also return to

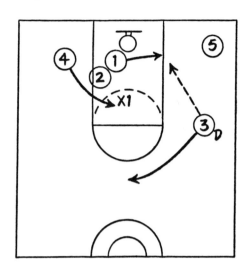

Diagram 3-21

their original positions. O_3 could then hit O_5 in Area 3 and the regular Drop-Step Play would continue as usual.

On occasion, however, O_4 cannot receive the ball because the man guarding O_1 or O_2 has not followed his man toward the base line and is clogging up the lane. We have found that a simple roll by O_1 or O_2 has often resulted in a clear opening underneath the basket (Diagram 3-21). Your players should be alert for this possibility before proceeding on with the Drop-Step Play.

Generally, however, O_4 should be able to receive the pass. Whether or not he is free for the ideal shot is another matter.

One move the defense can make which partially thwarts the play is to execute a switch. This will permit the uncontested jumper or lay-up, but it can often result in a mismatch. If O_4 has a definite mismatch, we encourage him to go to the basket as his first alternative. If nothing materializes, we will usually outlet the ball and pick up the attack from whatever area the outlet pass is received.

Another reason why O_4 may not have a clear scoring opportunity after receiving the pass is due to an improperly set pick. Ideally, the double pick should be set as low as possible and O_2 should be slightly outside O_1's pick (toward O_4) (Diagrams 3-19, 3-20, and 3-21 show this), or at least shoulder to shoulder with O_1's pick. Occasionally, O_2 will set his pick inside O_1 (away from O_4) (Diagram 3-22). This could allow O_4's man to slip over the top of the pick at least in good enough position to guard O_4 closely after the pass is received. It's also possible that the pick could be set too high. In this case, O_4 might receive the pass above the foul line.

This might be out of the shooting range of many big men who would normally play the base-line positions.

Whatever the reason, on occasion you will no doubt find 0₄ with the ball and no desirable shot or direct moves at hand. Though 0₄ can always outlet the ball to an open area, there is an easier alternative.

Since the ball is generally received near Area 4, 0₄ can simply move to Area 4 as shown in Diagram 3-23. From this point the Side-Drop-Step maneuver can be executed, with 0₃ and 0₅ forming the "marriage."

The principle of the bounce pass as a key has other possibilities as

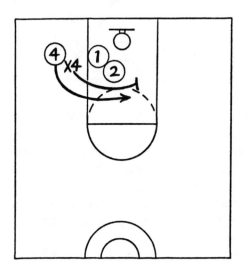

Diagram 3-22

Diagram 3-23

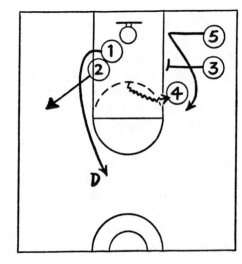

well. We have occasionally toyed with the idea of extending the bounce pass options on passes from Area 2 to Area 3. As shown in Diagram 3-24, the bounce pass to the corner would be followed by a double pick for O_2. It seems like a logical extension of the regular bounce pass principle.

However, you should be cautious about overextending yourself. Though the corner bounce pass is on the drawing board, we have not used it for one basic reason. Because of defensive overplays on the man moving to Area 3, we have found that the timing for a chest pass must be almost perfect to properly execute it. Therefore, a bounce pass is often employed to compensate for errors in timing since it is easier to handle. (We do not have the same difficulty on the wings since there are other ways of countering the overplay.) The bounce pass to Area 3 would have no value as a key if it were regularly employed in our standard movements. This would be a possibility, however, if you chose to explore it.

This same situation is true of the entire offense. With a little imagination, many other different play combinations could probably be developed.

However, to incorporate any more plays into the offense would defeat one of its major objectives—simplicity. Special plays might be devised for specific games, but generally we have found that the four plays outlined here have more than sufficed to see us through a season.

This is not to imply that no other play possibilities are better than the four described in this chapter. We, ourselves, are constantly experimenting with new situations. If we develop a play which definitely suits our purposes in a particular season, we will not hesitate to use it. However,

Diagram 3-24

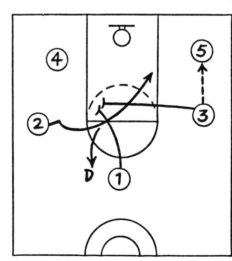

we may very likely also scrap one of the other plays for that season if we feel that the number of plays in the total system becomes unmanageable. In fact, the Side Drop Step is the most recent addition to the system, as it was not a part of the original play selections. It was incorporated only after it proved to complement the rest of the offense. In the process, a similar but less suitable play was eliminated.

Conversely, the corner bounce pass play was not installed because it could easily have interfered with other aspects of the total offense.

There is nothing magical about having four plays, nor is the number arbitrary. We have simply found that our players do not feel comfortable with any more than that. At this point we are really searching more for refinement of existing ways to use the Drop Step, for the offense is predicted on that move. There are only a limited number of ways and angles from which any maneuver can be effectively executed, especially without extraneous keys.

If you would devise new and better ways to use area keys, and if your team could handle a large variety of plays, then you would be foolish not to expand the offense.

Before being underwhelmed by the small play selection, however, bear this in mind. All of these plays can be run from both sides of the court with equal effectiveness. Therefore, without any contingent maneuvers, you have a minimum of eight plays. At least this is how it would appear to the defense. Add the planned and free-lance options, and you have a much greater variety of moves. Most basic maneuvers found in other plays can occur in this offense without breaking the basic patterns.

In addition, all of the plays presented here have been diagramed from a 1-2-2 formation. As you will see in a later chapter, the Drop-Step Play can be executed from almost any formation imaginable while the alternate plays can also be run from several alignments as well.

From a defensive standpoint, it's virtually impossible to calculate all of the numerous possibilities your offense presents.

Rebounding Position in the Area Key Offense

Before closing this chapter, one essential element of any successful offense must be explained in relation to the Area Key Offense —rebounding.

I'm not going to offer a long list of drills and techniques to enhance your team's rebounding ability. There are more than enough books which treat this subject much more adequately than I ever could hope to do. Nor am I going to expand upon my philosophy regarding the ultimate importance of rebounding in basketball. Let it be sufficient to say that I believe no matter how well-designed, organized, or executed an offense may be, a team which fails to hold its own on the offensive boards will come away on the losing end of the score in most contests.

Though we pride ourselves on taking only the good shot, this is certainly not enough to insure victory. Even a team which shoots 50% on the year (an abnormally high percentage) must realize that five out of every ten shots will miss the mark. In the average game, this means that 35 to 45 offensive rebounds will be up for grabs. Since each possession yields approximately 1 point for us statistically, every offensive rebound we can acquire represents a potential point in our favor. This is certainly reason enough to hit the boards with determination.

What is intended here is a description of how we *position* ourselves for rebounds on each of the various plays explained above. For the most part, the techniques we use for rebounding are the same as those traditionally employed in most other offenses.

Before explaining the positioning on plays run to completion, we must first consider those scoring opportunities which occur before a play is completed. If you're now acquainted with the potential of the offense, you must realize that this can be a common occurrence, and it must be anticipated. In general, we have a very simple rule for rebounding in such instances. When a shot is taken before the completion of a play, *everyone but the back guard* goes to the boards. If we are in a two-guard front, we designate beforehand which of the two will be considered the back guard. The other man goes for the "long rebound," establishing his position between the foul line and the dotted line of the foul circle in most cases. If we're in a single-guard formation, positioning will be determined by the nature of the shot taken. For example, a shot taken after a flash post move is shown in Diagram 3-25 ("R" denotes rebounder).

If O_4 flashes the lane, receives a pass from O_3, and shoots, the positioning is as follows. O_4 would naturally follow up his shot. O_5 would move in to the right base-line side of the basket and O_2 would cover the left side of the basket. O_3 would then move to the long rebounding position, since the desired triangle would already be established underneath. Of course if O_4 were effectively boxed out after the shot and O_3 beats his man to the lane, he should penetrate farther since the short shot will usually result in a short rebound. This type of thing comes with experience, however, and I doubt if any coach would effectively position his players perfectly on every shot without spending an undue amount of time accounting for every conceivable situation. Basic basketball sense

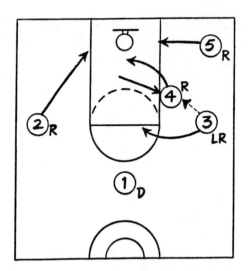

Diagram 3-25

and experience is of far greater importance in this respect than specific preparation. The important thing is that your rebounders are conditioned to be hungry for the ball and go for it. Court awareness will then come with experience.

We may adjust our rebounding positioning on these options depending upon the basic rebounding ability of our opponents and their style of play after they acquire the rebound. If they're a dominant team that likes to run, we may be a little cautious about crashing four men. If they're a strong rebounding team that seldom breaks, we will usually try to challenge them on the boards. A weak rebounding team usually will not even attempt the fast break since they must crash everyone just to stand a decent chance of securing the ball. This type of team might often find four-and-a-half of our rebounders hitting the boards, since our back guard may sneak into the foul line area with four full rebounders crashing.

However, whenever the Drop-Step Play is run to completion, we try to establish a rebounding triangle under the boards. By this, of course, is meant that the front and both sides of the basket are covered. Generally, the boards are not randomly crashed.

When the shot is taken off the drop step in Area 4, the triangle is established in a fairly predictable manner. If you will refer back to Diagram 3-6, you will note that O_1 has taken the shot off a screen by O_5. Normally, when O_5 moves to Area 4, his defender will try to stay between him and the basket to prevent O_5 from driving right on in for the score. In most cases, this defender will then be behind O_5 and slightly to his right-hand side when the screen is established. If his defender holds this position even after the drop step is made, O_5 should roll into the defender outside-in, keeping him inside. O_5 would then have adequate position to cover his right side of the board (Diagram 3-26). If O_5's defender steps out to hedge on O_1 after the drop step, the roll would be made in the opposite direction with the defender boxed out to the outside of the basket (Diagram 3-27).

Also in Diagram 3-26 you will note that the man not making the drop step (in this case, O_2) continues down the lane and sets a pick for O_4. This move is not just made to free O_4 inside for a possible scoring opportunity. If O_1 takes the shot, O_4 should also be free for better rebounding position underneath the basket.

If a switch is attempted on the pick, O_2's man, who is usually

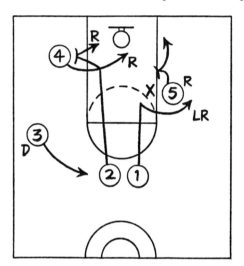

Diagram 3-26

Diagram 3-27

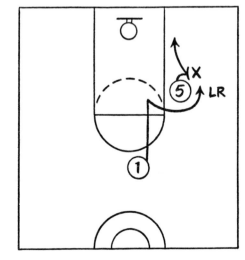

shorter, will be rebounding against one of your tallest men. If the switch does not occur, O_4 should be initially free to establish adequate positioning directly in front of the basket if O_1 takes the shot.

The weak side of the basket is covered by the man in the marriage not making the drop step (O_2 in Diagram 3-26). If the switch occurs, O_2 will have a taller man to rebound against. However, it is hoped that since his pick will give him the inside position, this might counter any disadvantage in height or rebounding ability. If the switch does not occur, there would naturally be a disadvantage on this side of the basket, but then O_4 should be free under the basket immediately and hopefully O_1 would spot him and make the pass.

In essence, then, while rebounding position is lost, an easy score is potentially gained.

Of course once O_1 takes the shot, he would follow his shot toward the middle for the long rebound.

Effective rebounding on the other plays must rely more on determination and court sense than on patterned positioning.

With the Scissors Play, the drop step can be made from either the side or the top. If the move is made from the side (Diagram 3-28), O_5 will roll on his defender outside-in since he will inevitably play O_5 behind and inside. O_3 will take the long rebound on the follow-up. O_4 and O_2 have the most difficult job. Since their defenders will probably be "sluffing off" between them and the ball, they must fight and maneuver for position, with O_4 taking the low position on the weak side of the basket and O_2 going for the position directly in front of the basket.

If the play is completed with O_1 making the drop step, the situation is slightly different. As shown in Diagram 3-24 earlier, O_3 would continue on to Area 2 opposite the ball if he does not receive the pass. O_2 would also replace O_1 in Area 1 (Diagram 3-29). Therefore, O_3 would assume the middle position in front of the basket. O_1 would follow into the long rebounding position, and O_4 would cover the low weakside position as in the first options. O_5 would have to read his defender and roll off him according to which side he positions himself, on the move by O_1. If he hedges toward O_1, the roll would be inside-out. If not, it would be the same as in the first option.

With the Side-Drop-Step Play, the weak side is almost entirely vacant except for the man in Area 2. The defense will vacate this side also, however, since they will follow the offense. Diagram 3-30 shows the positioning for this play.

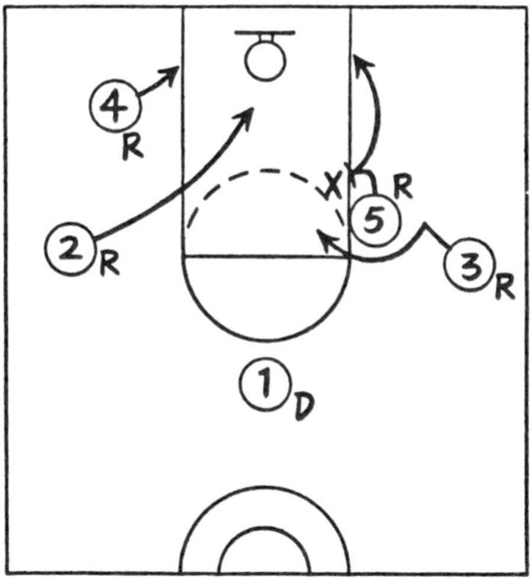

Diagram 3-28

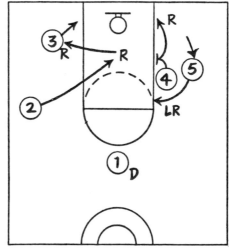

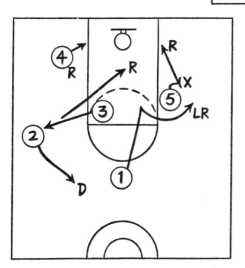

Diagram 3-29

Diagram 3-30

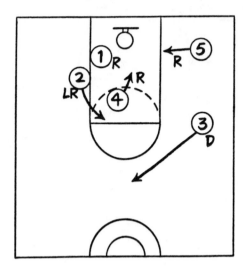

Diagram 3-31

As with the other plays, O_4 will roll to the ball side of the basket with the same rules in regard to his defender. O_3 will take the low weakside position, and O_2 would take the middle position in front of the basket. O_5 would follow for the long rebound.

In all of these plays, the man in Area 1 always remains as the back guard.

The Bounce Pass Play presents a slight departure from the usual format since the play itself is unlike the others in basic movement.

If O_4 does receive the pass from O_3 and takes the short jump shot, he would follow the shot. O_5, who had moved to the corner, would crash hard to establish the low position on his side of the basket. O_2 would roll to the middle and O_1 would cover low to his side. O_3 would move out to Area 1 as the back guard once the shot is taken. Diagram 3-31 shows the desired positioning.

If O_4 cannot shoot and sets up the Side-Drop-Step or regular Drop-Step Play, the rebounding would be the same as usual for these plays.

The positioning for plays run to the opposite side should simply be reversed.

There is one important factor you should bear in mind, though, regarding perfect positioning for rebounds with the offense. Since you can run the various plays from a number of different formations, it is impossible to always establish the exact positions diagramed from the 1-2-2 set. Therefore, we have tried to instill in our players the ability to recognize a logical connection between their place on the court and the rebounding position required of them in any particular instance. This is not as difficult as it may seem, for once you have developed the idea of the triangle around the basket, common court sense will usually dictate where the rebounders will go.

Some formations will naturally yield better intrinsic positioning than others, but none of the plays or formations would put you at an obvious disadvantage. They all contain the potential for adequate rebounding without any normal or exceptional maneuvering.

This will be seen more clearly when the various formations are presented later. Before explaining how to play multiple formation basketball, however, some time should first be taken to show how the key elements of this offense can be implemented.

4 | *How to Implement the Area Key Offense*

Acquainting Players with the Offense

In working with high school players from all parts of the country at summer basketball camps, one peculiarity has always stood out in my mind. While trying to understand the various playing styles of different boys in order to organize them into teams for the camp games, I often have had occasion to ask what type of offense they used at their high schools. Far more boys than you would expect are unable to answer meaningfully, many of them excellent players, technically. Each, however, obviously learned his own specific assignments and operated somewhat mechanically (though efficiently) within the context of the total offense. Either these boys did not understand the entire offensive system and the philosophy behind it, or they had horribly short memories. I tend to believe the former, since they often could remember specific plays.

Before seeking to operate the Area Key Offense, it is essential that your players understand the principles upon which it is based and the philosophy behind it. They must recognize the areas on the court, know their sequence, and realize how these areas are utilized in view of the total offensive system.

An important first step in implementing this offense, therefore, is to acquaint your team with the key areas.

Some coaches prefer to explain their strategies through the use of "chalk talks" or hand-out sheets. We do nearly all of our teaching on the court. This is especially significant with the Area Key Offense, since so much of its success depends upon the players having the "feel of the court," as well as a mental picture of their responsibilities.

To help acquaint your players with the key areas, you may use the rather simple but effective technique of taping out each area (described in Chapter 2) on the court for the first few days. These areas should also be numbered in proper sequence.

In fact, if you choose to utilize this technique, it may be wise to tape these areas on the court before the first practice session, without telling the players what they are or why they are there. In the first year of operation, this will serve to instill a sense of curiosity among team members. In subsequent years, only the new players in your program will be curious, but this will give the veterans a chance to refresh their own understanding since they will probably try to explain the purpose of the taped-out areas to the new members. It may also help to enhance their leadership ability and image in the eyes of the newcomers.

These areas will remain unexplained for several days, as most coaches spend the first week or so almost strictly on fundamental skills. This is certainly the place we begin, since no offense can even attempt to operate successfully without a reliance on basic skills.

Improving Your Passing Game

In listening to or conversing with various college coaches, the question that often arises is what factors most contribute to offensive ineffectiveness. One answer is almost universal, even among coaches of highly successful teams. Poor passing and pass catching cancels out more scoring opportunities than almost any other factor.

To improve our passing and pass catching, we have two drills which we alternate every other day for the entire season. The first of these is the Star Drill. As shown in Diagram 4-1, we form five lines around the foul circle (or mid-court circle). The man in line 1 passes to line 3 and goes to the left and rear of line 3. The receiver in line 3 then does the same with line 5, line 5 with line 2, line 2 with line 4, line 4 with line 1, etc. The

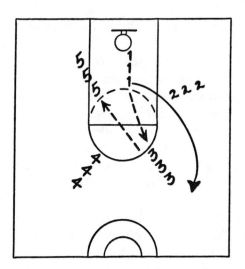

Diagram 4-1

process is continuous for one minute, and we try to complete 70 passes in this time. We subtract two for every muffed pass. You can encourage a sense of challenge by assessing penalty laps for everything under 70. Either a bounce pass or chest pass may be used. If we use a bounce pass, we lower the goal to 50.

This drill not only encourages accurate passing and adept pass catching, but also adds one other important factor to the passing game—going to meet the ball. All passers are in motion when the passes are made, and all pass catchers are moving toward the ball when the pass is caught.

The second drill we use is the Split Vision Drill. As shown in Diagram 4-2, our players line up in a semi-circle with one man in the center. The center man has one ball, as does the first man in the perimeter. The center man passes to the second man in the circle to start the drill, and the first man in the circle simultaneously passes to the man in the center. This process continues around the entire perimeter and back again. This process must be completed without any errors in passing or catching by the man in the center before he is replaced. All passes must be as crisp as possible.

This drill serves several purposes. First, it encourages the use of peripheral vision. Secondly, the man in the center especially must have "good hands" and a quick release. He must also have strength, as the arms get quite tired if the first round proves unsuccessful. Furthermore, the drill encourages accuracy in passing, as the players in the perimeter are told to always return a good pass. A poor pass by the center man will require recovery before the ball is returned. This time delay may mean that two balls will fly back at this center man at once. At the very least,

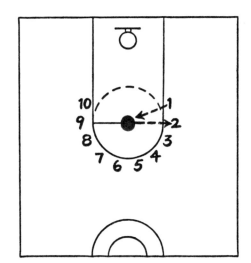

Diagram 4-2

he'll drop one. More than likely he'll be forced to take a "shot" in the chest or elsewhere. Only with good, crisp passes and good pass catching can the drill be completed successfully. Out of a sense of self-preservation, if nothing else, even the worst passers and receivers become competent enough to make it through on the first round after a few weeks. We have found that these two drills adequately serve our purposes. You may have special drills of your own which accomplish these same goals.

Of course, many drills for other purposes also require the ball to be passed. Regardless of how incidental passing may be to the operation of these drills, we insist that *all* passes be executed properly at all times. Sloppy passing in shooting or rebounding drills will undoubtedly have an adverse carry-over effect.

Teaching the Drop-Step Maneuver

Besides the bounce pass and chest pass, there is one other type of pass which is instrumental to the operation of our offense—the simple hand-off. However, since this pass is used almost exclusively to complete the basic play, we employ a drill which also teaches two other skills essential to the offense—the drop-step maneuver and the shot off the drop step. This drill also gives us practice in moving the ball from Area 3 to Area 4 on the dribble. I would highly recommend it.

As shown in Diagram 4-3 the man in line 2 dribbles from Area 3 to Area 4 and establishes his position. As soon as he is set, the man in line 1 heads down the lane below the screen and executes the drop-step ma-

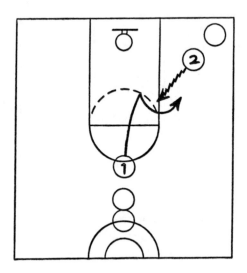

Diagram 4-3

neuver. O_2 gives O_1 the hand-off and O_1 shoots the short jumper. O_2 then spins off for the rebound and O_1 follows his shot for the long rebound. The ball is then passed to line 2 and the drill continues. O_1 goes to the end of line 2 and O_2 goes to the end of line 1. This drill should be run to both sides of the court.

Originally this drill is done without opposition, but after the players have mastered these movements the drill can be run "live." Also, another line can later be added at the top of the circle to more closely approximate the realistic situation.

Though this drill seems quite simple, it incorporates many of the basic elements of the Drop-Step Play, and care should be exercised to make certain that these elements are properly implemented.

First, for the men in line 2, the move from Area 3 to Area 4 should be as direct as possible. The ball handler has only four seconds to control the ball on a dribble. He must learn to dribble adequately with his outside hand, in this case the left hand. He must then be sure to position himself properly in Area 4. If he is too far up the lane, the shot will be longer than we want. If he is too low, the area near the basket will be too congested for any option maneuvers to succeed. Here is where taping the area on the court usually proves quite useful.

Next, care should be taken to insure that the hand-off is securely made. The man receiving the pass cannot be forced too far away from the ball as the defender could possibly step in between the ball and the shooter. Nor is the short hand-off as easy to execute as it appears. Fumbles are quite frequent if this move is not practiced regularly. The screener should set his feet wide apart for a larger screen, and he must be careful to protect the ball at all times.

For the man in line 1, the drop-step move must be accomplished with proper footwork for maximum effectiveness. The man must, first of all, be sure to go below the potential screen before starting back around. When he is ready to execute the drop step, the foot farthest from the ball should be planted firmly before pushing-off to move back around the screen. Once he steps around for the hand-off, he must come as close to the ball as possible. He will virtually take the ball from the screener. Once he has the ball, the receiver should be in a position to shoot without taking a dribble or traveling. This is most easily done if he takes a slight jumping step just before the hand-off is made and hits the floor with both feet after receiving the ball. Since many players like to shoot off the dribble, this move will take time to perfect.

If two men are coming down the lane together and the outside man will execute the drop step, you must be sure that he goes slightly below his partner, who stops even with the ball, before making the move. In that way, he will have a double screen from which to maneuver for the shot (Diagram 4-4). The drop-step move from this position is the same as noted above.

You should also execute this same drill from other angles on the court, as the alternate plays are run in this maneuver. (See Diagram 4-5).

This drill is specifically designed for our own unique purposes. We also spend a great deal of time on perfecting other more general fundamental skills, since most of our contingent maneuvers are quite basic.

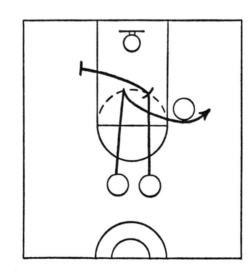

Diagram 4-4

Diagram 4-5

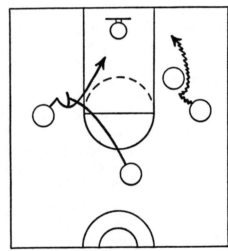

Diagram 4-6

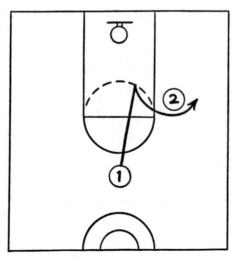

Diagram 4-7

Teaching Basic Offensive Skills

One of these skills involves moving without the ball. Though our primary plays involve screens set to the ball, we feel that our movements away from the ball are really what keep the defense honest. We, therefore, have a simple drill that teaches basic cuts and picks away from the ball.

For the purpose of clarity, I should first mention that we use the terms "picks" and "screens" as representing two different entities. We define a pick as a movement designed to free a man from his defender so that he can receive a pass and move in for the score *away* from the man who rubbed off his defender. The term screen is used only when one man uses another as a sort of wall behind which he can shoot unmolested by a defender.

In Diagram 4-6 picks are set, since the scoring opportunity would occur *away* from the man rubbing off the defender. In Diagram 4-7, O_1 is using O_2 as a wall behind which he will shoot. Therefore, this is a screen by our definition.

Though many coaches use these terms synonymously, we make the distinction for a very simple reason. Our screens are held longer than picks, and we seldom roll off a screen. With today's pressure defense as advocated by coaches like Al La Balbo and Bobby Knight gaining more acceptance, we find that many teams are reluctant to "switch." They will fight *over* the top of a screen. In such instances, a roll is really quite futile. We feel, therefore, that it is better to hold our screens as long as possible and settle for the jumper.

Another reason results from player responsibilities. We like our picks set to the side and slightly to the rear with a wide stance. This is the responsibility *of the man setting the pick.* In our screens, we simply ask that our screener assume a wide stance. It is up to the other man to work his defender into or behind the screener.

Therefore, when we call for a pick or screen during a game, our players know exactly what we mean.

As I mentioned earlier, our basic play involves a screen, but we also have a simple drill whereby we work on picks and cuts.

In Diagram 4-8, we have three lines which approximate our offense when the ball has entered Area 2. In the first phase, we ask O_2 to pass the ball to O_3 to begin the movement. After the pass is made, he then executes a simple give-and-go. This may take one of two forms. First, he can start away from the ball and then cut between his (imaginary) defender and the

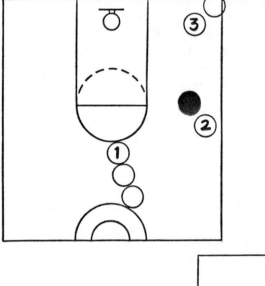

Diagram 4-8

Diagram 4-9

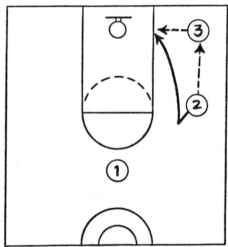

ball (Diagram 4-9). Secondly, he can move toward the ball and then go behind the defender for the common backdoor cut (Diagram 4-10). Both of these moves are standard options in our basic play, and the importance of making a proper cut should be greatly emphasized. He should never make a "straight cut," and he should move as quickly as possible to free himself. You should also stress the importance of a good return pass by 0_3.

Next we ask that 0_2 set a pick for 0_1, after he passes to 0_3 (Diagram 4-11). Three things should be stressed here. First, make sure that 0_2 sets a proper pick. Then make certain that 0_1 takes a first step away from the pick and then back around it. This will make it easier to rub off the defender. Lastly, stress the good return pass to the cutter.

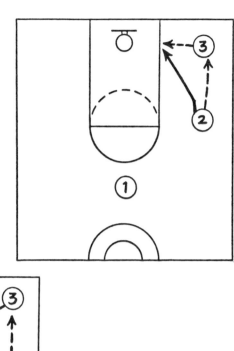

Diagram 4-10

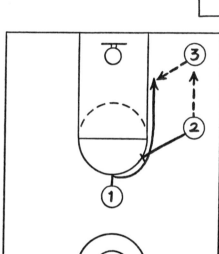

Diagram 4-11

After all lines have rotated, you can have O₂ execute a roll to the basket in case you do encounter a switching team (Diagram 4-12).

Once the players have become acquainted with these basic moves, you may run the drill with defenders.

This same drill can be run from other positions on the court as well (Diagram 4-13), and you can also add a fourth position (Diagram 4-14).

In Diagram 4-14, you will notice that O₂ may set a pick for O₄ after hitting O₃. This pick may be stationary, but we have found that O₄ can more easily free himself if he heads across the lane as O₂ is making his regular cut through the lane. O₄ simply rubs his man off on O₂ on the way across. Though this could constitute a moving pick, few officials will call it if O₂ does not go out of his way to set this pick. They will usually

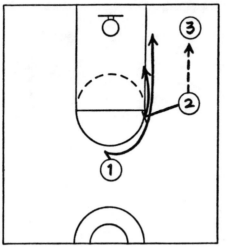

Diagram 4-12

Diagram 4-13

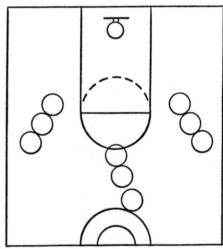

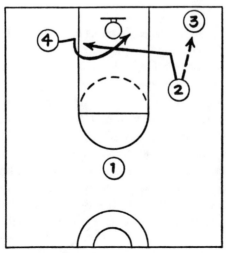

Diagram 4-14

concede him a normal path. It is up to O_4, of course, to use O_2's cut to his advantage.

You may find that variations of these movement drills suit your own purposes better, or you may have your own drills for accomplishing these same ends. However, we have a very simple philosophy regarding a large number of our drills. We try to make them approximate the real situations of our offense as closely as possible, whenever applicable. In any event, the critical point is that you realize the importance of perfecting these basic offensive skills before expecting this or any offense to function smoothly.

Next, we come to one of the controversial facets of offensive basketball—the 1-on-1 moves. Some coaches swear by 1-on-1 moves, while others feel they are a disruptive influence on team play. Without wishing to get involved in any philosophical discussion of this matter, let me just say that in the Area Key Offense there are many opportunities which arise for 1-on-1 moves to prove effective, if you choose to use them.

For this reason, we have felt that we should spend an adequate amount of time teaching basic individual maneuvers with the ball from the various key areas. Only the more universal moves taught with our basic skills are presented here. Those moves, intricately connected with our offense, as well as moves for the big men inside, are presented later in the chapters on free-lancing and countering defensive adjustment.

These 1-on-1 moves are taught as a series, with each one contingent upon or as a follow-up to the previous movement to capitalize on defensive adjustments.

In all of our individual maneuvers, we want our players to do three basic things. First, we want them to receive the ball in an area within their shooting range. In that way, if the defender sluffs off, preventing any subsequent move without resorting to a dribble, we can take the shot he gives us. Also, the ball should be received in such a way that the receiver can see what is going on about him (if a man breaks free, if a defender stumbles, etc.). He should not have his back to the basket upon reception, and we would prefer he did not have to declare a pivot foot before he begins his move. This is best accomplished if the receiver takes a short hop and spins as he receives the ball. Then he will be facing the basket with either foot as a pivot foot. Secondly, if possible, we want the ball held in the chest area so we can easily shoot, pass, or dribble. Lastly, when a move is made toward the basket, the first step should be directly toward the basket, taking as few dribbles as possible to reach the basket.

The first of these individual moves is the simple Step-Stop-and-Go. In this maneuver, the offensive man takes a short jab step toward the basket. If the defender holds or reacts with a backward step that puts him off-balance, the offensive man turns on the speed and blows past him.

There are two counter-moves to this. The first is the cross-over step. If the defender overreacts in the direction of the first step, the man crosses over with his lead foot and goes to the basket. The second counter-move is the Step-Back-and-Shoot. In this move, if the defender takes the initial fake and retreats noticeably, the man with the ball simply steps back and takes the jumper. Also, if the defender lunges hard toward the ball, trying to recover, he can fake and drive past him.

The last basic move in the series is the Rocker Step. In this move we lead forward, like the previous move, but instead of pulling back all the way, we simply throw the head and shoulders back. When the defender reacts to this fake, we continue on to the basket.

To practice these moves, we simply incorporate them into our regular warm-up drill. Instead of having two lines merely shooting lay-ups, we go through each of these moves first and then drive in for the lay-up (except for the move with the jump shot). This drill is used every other day in practice and also in pre-game or halftime warm-ups.

Naturally, we use many drills besides these to teach other fundamental aspects of basketball. Those presented here are the ones most useful and most in harmony with the principles of the Area Key Offense. Though we use most of these drills regularly during the season, we concentrate on them most heavily in the first two weeks of the season. After our staff is satisfied that we have achieved at least some degree of competence in the basic skills, we then move on to an explanation of our total offensive system.

Installing the Actual Offense

At that time, we are ready to explain the meaning of the areas marked out on the court. By now the players should be aware of the location of each of these areas. We tell the players that the entire effectiveness of our offense depends upon their recognition of these areas and their sequence. The concept of "live areas" is then explained. You can illustrate this concept with a very simple drill.

As shown in Diagram 4-15, you can have your team line up in a tight 1-2-2 formation, with the ball near the mid-court circle. As the ball enters Area 1, have your players nearest Area 2 break to that area on each side.

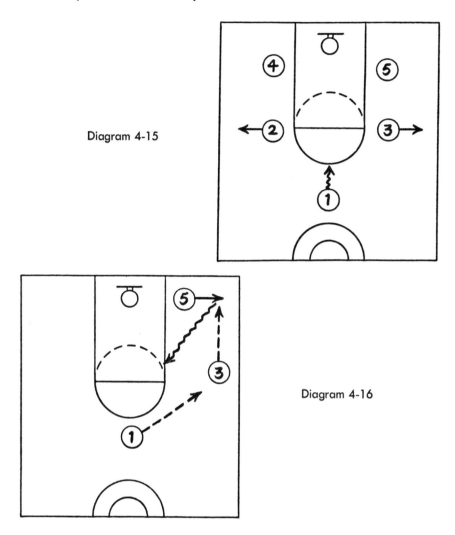

Diagram 4-15

Diagram 4-16

In this case it is O_2 and O_3. When the ball enters Area 2, the man nearest Area 3 should break to that area (Diagram 4-16). Once the ball is advanced to Area 3, the man receiving the pass should then dribble the ball to Area 4, as in the Drop-Step Play.

After you've done this with a 1-2-2 formation, you can try the same drill from a 1-3-1 formation, double stacks, and triangles shown in Diagrams 4-17, 4-18, and 4-19. Be sure to run each of these drills from both sides of the court.

Once you're sure that the players have "the feel" of these areas, you can remove the tape and run these same drills again. Stay away from two-guard formations at first, as Area 1 is often unoccupied in these sets,

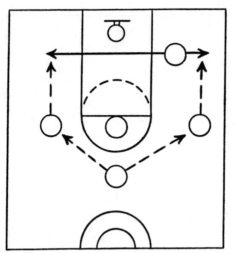

Diagram 4-17

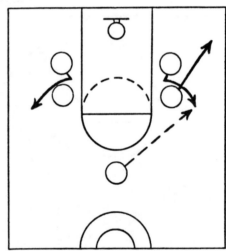

Diagram 4-18

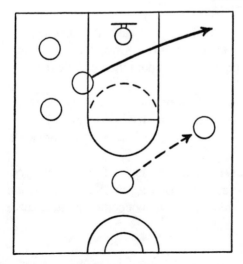

Diagram 4-19

and this necessitates area by-passes. Generally we feel it is easier to teach the basic movements without going into exceptions to the rules. These can come later.

At this time it would be more advisable to go directly into an explanation of the Drop-Step Play, as the previous drill has given your team most of the basic movements necessary for its completion.

We have found it best to first teach the Drop-Step Play from the 1-2-2 formation, and though we explain that certain options are available, we ask that they run the play only to the point where the jump shot is taken in Area 4. When we are satisfied with the timing and basic movements, we will then teach the play from the other single-guard formations. The play should always be run from both sides.

After this is done, you can go back and install the two-guard formations—the 2-1-2 and 2-2-1. Before doing this, it must first be explained how an area can be by-passed and then show how the ball can be advanced to an area with a dribble. (Chapter 2 explains this.) Basically, the same drill as mentioned above can be used with minor alterations as shown in Diagram 4-20. You can then install the play from these formations.

Once your players know how to complete the play to the point of the drop step, you can then cover those planned options which can occur before and afterward. You can also designate the proper rebounding positions at this time.

It should be noted that all of these installments are made without any defensive opposition. Only after we are certain that our players fully understand their responsibilities will we run the plays "live."

Diagram 4-20

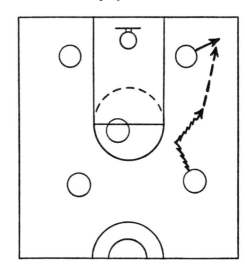

Obviously, when you begin to run your plays "live," with your own team members on defense, they try to get cute and play the pattern rather than their men. Many coaches find that their offense suffers accordingly when the defense knows the plays. Some ask that the defenders try to play it "honest" so the offense can function more smoothly. We make no such requests.

As you will see in Chapter 6, our offense has many ways of countering defensive adjustments. Whenever we feel the defense has gained the upper hand, this gives us a natural opportunity to stop the action, go over each of these defensive adjustments, and point out how they can be avoided or overcome. Since the players will encounter similar maneuvers by the defense in game conditions, we feel that this is a more realistic way to approach the problem.

Usually simple counter-moves within the context of the play will suffice at first, but gradually this will lead you into a perfect opportunity for installing the alternate plays. Once you begin teaching these plays, you can use the same format for instruction as with the Drop-Step Play.

The last method of counter-attack we teach is the use of various free-lance options. This is done only after we are sure that the basic plays can be properly executed. By nature, the number of free-lance options are virtually infinite, since they operate under various conditions of time and place. However, almost all of these options are based upon a few fundamental movements which are usually covered in the opening sessions of practice. In addition to these basic movements, we spend time showing specific moves from each of the various positions on the court. These are explained in Chapter 7. Since all of our free-lance options occur within the context of the various plays, we are not so apprehensive as some teams about relying on them. If they break down, we can always go back to our established plays. If you use the free-lance options, you will find that as the season progresses your own unique personnel characteristics will favor some moves over others, and you will come to rely most heavily on them. Certain opponents may also require specific options. So, generally speaking, the offense's use of free-lancing is not as helter-skelter as the term might imply to some coaches.

Once the free-lance options have been implemented, your offense is virtually complete. From this point on, defensive adjustments can, in fact, be encouraged as they are usually quite futile and actually serve to give confidence to the offense. We have found that after being "burned" on numerous occasions, our defense will usually decide to play it honest.

Organizing Your Practices

To arrive at this stage, the entire process takes about ten days, devoting about one hour of practice time each day to man-for-man offense. Ideally, the schedule would be as follows:

1st day—Area Recognition and Movement Drill from single-guard formations.

2nd day—Drop-Step Play from single-guard formations.

3rd day—Area Recognition Drill from two-guard formations—Drop-Step Play from two-guard formations.

4th day–Drop-Step Play run live from various formations;
        &   countering defensive adjustments.
5th day

6th day—Alternate plays installed from each formation applicable.
7th day
    &
8th day
9th day—Free-lance options installed.
    &
10th day

This schedule would hold true only if you chose to adopt the entire system. If you simply wanted to install the idea of area keys with the drop-step play alone, you could do this in a relatively short time, especially if you cut down on the number of formations used.

As you may have perceived by now from looking at the diagrams, our fundamental drills are run with varied numbers of players. Once we begin to install our offense, however, we invariably practice as a five-man unit. 1-on-1 and 3-on-3 drills are fine in their place, but basketball is a five-man game—and we believe, in general, it should be approached in that manner. At least we have found this to be the case in terms of implementing the Area Key Offense. Since the start of every play potentially involves each and every member of the team in a scoring opportunity, we find there is no substitute for allotting a large portion of the practice time to working as a five-man unit. Furthermore, once the entire offense is implemented, we practice live almost entirely and take any scoring opportunities which arise. If the coaches feel that we are becoming too patterned in any given session (too much to one side, too much of one formation, too much reliance on a particular move, etc.), we simply call the offensive team together and explain how we want the offense varied.

The only time we do not go live is if we wish to work on a special plan of attack for a particular game, or if we feel the team is in need of a "refresher course."

How much practice time should you allot to the Area Key Offense? That is mainly a matter of choice, dependent upon your own standards of perfection, personnel, style of play of the opponents in your conference, etc. I can only tell you what schedule we have found to be most successful. Generally, our practice sessions last about two hours. During this time, we spend approximately 80 minutes working as a five-man unit, with equal time devoted to offense and defense. The 40 minutes devoted to offense is used in different ways depending on our particular upcoming opponent. We usually divide the time equally between zone and man-for-man offense, but we may concentrate solely on either of these phases. Some days we may not practice the Area Key Offense at all. However, we do not like to go too long without working on it as our movements may become stale. Therefore, we usually try to schedule the Area Key Offense at least a few minutes each day, even if we greatly expect to see a zone defense.

However, one of the biggest difficulties we face in determining our practice schedule is that of limited facilities. There are three gymnasiums available in our district. Competing for the use of those gyms are a junior high school team, a freshman team, the junior varsity and varsity squads, and a girl's basketball team. The varsity and junior varsity teams always practice at the high school gym where our games are played. For this reason, we are forced to practice together. Some schools have the varsity and junior varsity practice at different times, one in the afternoon and one in the evening. This is impossible in our situation as our junior high and freshman teams use the high school gym for their games. This gym is also used for wrestling matches. If a night is available, the girls usually try to hold a practice session at that time, since they also play their games at the high school.

In addition, being a rural school district, few of our athletes live near enough to the school to walk to practice. Transportation, therefore, becomes a problem with regular night sessions.

If you face no such problems, you have my blessing. With expanded athletic programs appearing nationwide, however, I believe that our situation is more the rule than the exception. More than likely, a majority of you coaches are compelled to share your practice sessions with another team as we do.

If these conditions apply in your case, much of your practice time is spent on a half-court. In practicing half-court, we have adopted a slightly unusual format. Though we do alternate regularly to get the feel of both halves of the court and both baskets, we usually spend more time at one basket than the other. The reason for this is quite simple. Over a course of several years, we have found that our opponents overwhelmingly choose the basket near the clock for the second half. Rightly or wrongly, our players feel that some baskets are better than others, and they would rather have the "hot" basket for the second half. For this reason, we spend a little more practice time at the basket away from the clock and *make* it our "hot" basket. This is the basket we usually occupy for the second half. This feeling may be unique with our team. However, I tend to feel that many teams have their own idiosyncrasies which may require similar adjustments. In any event, though we shoot an adequate percentage in the first half, we have been known as a second-half team, especially at home.

The technique we use for practicing our offense half-court is the one we have found to be most successful. We scrimmage live and do not constantly alternate between offense and defense. Our first unit stays on offense for a given period of time (usually 20 minutes), and we work a sixth and possibly seventh man into the scrimmage at various intervals. To add a sense of competition, we often ask the offense to score a given number of baskets in the allotted time period. As soon as a basket is scored or the defense gets the ball, it is quickly returned and we begin our attack again. If we wish to work on our controlled offensive game, we drop the scoring requirements. As soon as the allotted time is exhausted, we switch over to defense and our second unit takes the attack.

When the scoring requirement is in effect, we discourage unnecessary fouling by assessing a penalty basket for every two fouls. Deliberate stalling by the defense is eliminated by giving more time to the offense. You may use a stop-watch to accomplish this same purpose.

Naturally, we recognize that there are limitations to practicing half-court, since basketball is a full-court game. However, since we are forced to spend an inordinate amount of time on a half-court, our strategy is designed to force our opponents to play the game a half-court at a time, both offensively and defensively. We seldom fast break, and rarely allow opponents to do so. If we are "pressed," we take only the lay-up or else set up our offense once we pass mid-court.

We feel that the Area Key Offense is very easily adapted to such a game plan, and we have no trouble implementing it on a half-court basis.

If you prefer a full-court strategy and have the facilities to adequately practice your game plan on this basis, the Area Key Offense can be equally effective. In fact, you will see in Chapter 7 that this offense is quite compatible with a fast break attack and can be used in conjunction with it, or as a continuation of fast break movements.

This discussion is not to imply that we practice solely on a half-court basis. We always reserve at least 20 minutes at the end of our practice sessions for full-court use. Occasionally, the varsity and junior varsity square off, but most often the first and second units of the varsity take possession of the court.

When this happens, we may do several different things. First, we may practice our press offense and defense one phase at a time, especially if we plan to use them against our next opponent. Secondly we may use the full court simply for a regular scrimmage game, concentrating on those areas of our attack which are the weakest. Such scrimmages are necessary, of course, just to get the feel of actual game conditions and demands. The third thing we may do is have our second unit imitate as closely as possible the characteristic style of play of certain opponents. We then conduct our scrimmage as if we were playing our next game. We may also take the full court for a longer time and combine the first and third technique if our opponent warrants it.

I think you will find that this amount of full-court usage is sufficient to prepare your team for the games. If the gymnasium is available long enough on Saturdays, you can stagger your sessions, with the varsity and junior varsity getting about an hour-and-a-half to themselves. In such instances, you can use the full court almost the entire time. This should certainly give you enough of an opportunity to familiarize the team with actual game conditions.

Actually, though, we've been practicing half-court so long and have so geared our philosophy to the half-court style of play, that even if a full court were always available, I believe we would still spend a large portion of our time practicing just as we do now. When you're forced to live with something for a long enough time, you begin to find ways to use the situation to your advantage. In retrospect, as our style of play now stands, we're probably no worse off with our limited facilities than we would be under better physical circumstances. We do what we have to, and we're good at what we do.

Now, in summary, I will briefly review the phases suggested for implementing the Area Key Offense.

First, devote your initial practice sessions to teaching sound fundamental skills necessary to operate the offense. The drills you use to perfect these skills should be periodically used throughout the season to insure that the skills are sharp and permanently developed.

Secondly, the players must be aware of the principles upon which the offense is based and the tremendous potential it affords. This is best accomplished through a step-by-step approach to each facet, logically linking one to the other. In essence, you *build* the offense rather than insert it.

Finally, spend a large portion of your practice time working as a unit on the basic plays and options. Since each play involves every player as a potential scorer, it is only logical that you should practice as an entire team.

We have found this format most suitable for our purposes. If your own use of the Area Key Offense warrants otherwise, you should definitely adopt the method of implementation which best fits your needs.

For instance, if you choose to use area keys based on your own plays, your introductory drills should be geared to your own basic movements. Also, if you feel you do not have the personnel to utilize all of the formations given, it would be foolish to practice any others than those formations which match your team's personality. Likewise, if you do not feel that you can use all of the phases of the attack described above, you should eliminate those which are not applicable and concentrate only on those you plan to use regularly. You can always institute special plays or options for specific games.

It would be easy for me to suggest that you at least try to implement all of the phases of the offense as we do. Obviously, I believe in all of what we do, for if they were not successful, I would abandon the useless portions.

However, you know your team best. If you have a feeling that certain phases of our attack won't work for you, there is little sense in wasting valuable time trying to implement them.

Nevertheless, I do feel confident that this offense is versatile enough that you can use much of what is presented here, regardless of your personnel.

5 | *How to Play Multiple Formation Basketball*

Theory Behind Multiple Formations

For a moment I would like to digress from the subject of basketball to a brief discussion of some trends in football.

Partially because football is played a phase at a time, there seems to be a greater amount of emphasis and analysis devoted to the segmented aspects of offense and defense. Coaches, commentators, and spectators are therefore much more aware of the particular types of offenses and defenses employed by various teams.

Under conditions of intense publicity, it is not difficult to see why certain offenses would catch the attention of a wide audience. As with many other elements of our culture exposed to the mass media, it is not unusual to expect the development of a fad.

This certainly appears to be the case with offensive systems in football. A certain offensive system yields spectacular results for a particular team, and suddenly it seems that everyone is ready to adopt it.

However, this is not really the case. It's merely an illusion created by media overkill. Contrary to popular opinion, at one time or another all coaches have not gone to the Slot, I, or Wishbone formations. Some never tried any of them, and others only "toyed" with each as a part of their offense.

One fact does remain, however. Throughout all the "fad" periods, one system has always maintained its popularity—the Multiple Formation Offense. And the reasons for this are quite simple.

Great talent can make moderately potent specialized offenses seem unbeatable. Unfortunately, by definition, teams with great talent are few and far between. Most coaches can't afford the luxury of a highly specialized offense which requires exceptional talent at specific positions in order to make the system function smoothly and effectively. Nor can they afford to make a total commitment to a style of play, which, if unsuccessful, eliminates the possibility of employing an alternate attack. If you choose to live or die with a specialized offense, you better not have the personnel that rolls over and dies easily.

With a Multiple Formation Offense, however, ordinary talent can operate it effectively, while superior talent can make it proportionally more effective.

Whenever the impact of an offense boils down to the element of pure physical confrontation and/or superb execution, superior talent will prevail. However, once you add the ingredients of disguise, unpredictability, and deception, you may easily have found the great equalizer. These are the elements of attack that multiple formations have to offer—disguise, unpredictability, and deception in the form of variety.

The theory behind Multiple Formation Offense is quite simple and quite sound. If you run four plays from one formation, you have merely presented the defense with four situations to counter. However, if it's possible to run these same four plays from five different formations, you have given your opponent 20 situations to defense.

Of course, even a single formation team can run 20 separate plays, but consider the burden this places on the players' memories. It's much easier to learn four plays and five formations than 20 separate assignments.

Such variety affords a distinct advantage. How does one prepare a game plan designed to stop such a wide range of scoring opportunities? Normally game plans are drawn on the basis of scouting reports, but

Multiple Formation Offense causes considerable difficulty to scouts in several respects.

In any one game, a limited number of plays may be run from several different formations. But what does this tell the scout about your offense? Even if he is adept, all he knows is that you can run any one of several plays from any one of several formations, which is next to nothing in a definite sense.

Since each formation presents its own special problems aside from set plays, opponents would have to be briefed on how to play the formations themselves. Then the plays themselves, each run from a different angle or area, would have to be covered. Even if adequate preparation could be made (which is highly doubtful), it would almost negate working on any other phases of the game other than defense.

Conversely, suppose you found a particularly limited attack successful in a certain game. Let's suppose you ran only one play from several formations or a few different plays from one formation. Any coach with a decent team has to assume he's being scouted. All he has to do is alter this previous trend in the next game. If you ran one play from several formations, you could run different plays the next game. Or if only one formation was used in one game, you could alter your formation in the next game. If you are scouted over a number of games, the net result of the reports is that you can run several plays from several formations.

You will have either eliminated the possibility of special preparations by your opponents or given them false information as to the extent of your offensive variety. In the former case, you can concentrate on a team's natural weakness. (Almost every team has some weakness you can exploit.) In the latter case, you can capitalize on artificial weaknesses caused by overadjustment on the part of the defense designed to stop a limited portion of your offense.

If you can guard against extreme tendencies to run specific plays from certain formations, prior scouting is virtually useless. You will always remain an unpredictable opponent. During a game this is also true, as your opponents cannot confidently gamble on risky, on-the-spot adjustments.

Why Multiple Formations Are Possible

Being sound in theory does not make an offense practical, however. Having played and coached football for many years, I was well aware of the potential advantages of such a system. But there are some considerable differences between football and basketball. In basketball there is no secrecy of the huddle for calling either formations or plays, and there is very little time to digest the assignments of a play once it's called. Movement is almost spontaneous. There are time-outs and breaks in action on fouls, but they are far too infrequent to rely upon for the basis of an attack.

The major problem, therefore, is in keying such an offense. Since by now you should be familiar with the idea of area keys and the various plays in our offense, you should be able to see why such a system allows multiple formations to operate.

There is really no reason to call out a formation since the players could line up at random and the basic play could still be run in reference to areas. There is no reason to call the plays either, since the movements of the players in or out of the areas dictate what will be run. If, and when, a particular formation or set of formations are felt to be desirable for a certain game, they can be designated beforehand or during a break in the action. Otherwise, you can simply play it "by ear."

If the theory of Multiple Formation Offense appears sound to you, but you are still somewhat skeptical about its potential for basketball, the remainder of this chapter should convince you that it is indeed a realistic proposition. All of the play possibilities presented here have been tested under game conditions. There is nothing spectacular about them.

The Drop-Step Play from Various Formations

In Chapter 3, all of the plays were diagramed from a 1-2-2 formation for simplicity's sake. It is now time to examine some other possibilities.

First we will look at some formations which utilize the single-guard approach, the same as a 1-2-2 does. These formations can be designated before the ball approaches mid-court, or the players can move into them from other formations without too much difficulty. For instance, a 1-2-2 can easily become a 1-4 formation if the base-line men move up into a mid or high post on each side of the lane as the wing men break out. A 1-2-2 can easily become a stack also if the formation is packed in tight along the lane with the back-line men breaking out to the wings. We have also used the 1-2-2 as a basis for moving to a 1-3-1 by simply bringing up one of the base-line men to a high post at the foul line.

If you are playing your opponent deliberately, there probably isn't much advantage in switching from one formation into the other. However, if you feel you can move in for the quick strike, the movement from one formation to another may cause a temporary confusion upon which you can capitalize, especially if your opponent is used to playing you in one particular formation for a considerable period of time. A defender may have become accustomed to playing your biggest man as a low post or base-line man in a 1-2-2 set. If he is a capable defensive player, he will probably also adjust quickly if his man comes down before the ball reaches mid-court and sets himself in a high post. However, a quick move from a low to a high post may not give him the time he needs to think and adjust, especially if the offense moves along quickly in its normal pattern. Where he had to watch for a flash into the post from the weak side or a move to the corner, he now has to play a post man who rolls to the basket on the strong side. And all of it can happen so quickly from a switch in formations!

In any event, regardless of what formation you use, the plays will still generally proceed along the lines of the basic principles already outlined. Certain formations require some alterations from these principles, but the rules in regard to the areas remain unaltered.

Though you could probably use a new formation in a game without having worked on it previously, it is generally wise to cover each potential formation in advance because of these slight alterations.

As you will see later in this chapter, all of the plays cannot be run from all formations without unduly straining the simplicity of the offense. Though the Drop-Step Play is virtually universal in regard to formations, some of the other plays are limited as to which formations can be successfully used to execute them. These will be explained as they arise.

Each play will be discussed as it is run from the various formations.

Diagram 5-1 shows a 1-3-1 alignment, with base-line man O_4 having moved up to a high post. It is fairly easy to execute the Drop-Step Play from this formation as Area 2 is already occupied on both sides. If the rules were strictly followed, regardless of which side the point guard hit, O_5 would move to Area 3 on that side. However, we have altered this rule slightly to take advantage of our personnel capabilities and to capitalize on or exploit defensive weaknesses. The side with no base-line man is designated as our "1-on-1 side." In Diagram 5-1, it is O_2's side. If the pass goes to O_2, there will be no immediate movement to Area 3 on his side by O_5. O_2 first has the option of going 1-on-1 against his man. If the defender is weak or in foul trouble, and O_2 has good individual moves, this option can prove to be quite advantageous.

O_5 gives O_2 a count of two to make a definite move. If O_2 does not

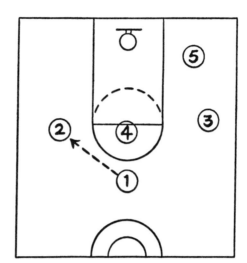

Diagram 5-1

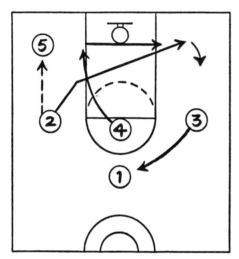

Diagram 5-2

beat his man in this time, O_5 will move across the base line to Area 3. If O_3 is given the pass, O_5 would go to Area 3 on his side, automatically.

Regardless of the side hit, once the ball is passed to Area 3, the movements are as shown in Diagram 5-2. Assuming O_2 could not move effectively 1-on-1, he would pass to O_5 in Area 3. O_2 would then clear the side as usual. However, the presence of O_4 so near Area 4 would be too congested to operate any maneuvers effectively. Therefore, we ask that the high post—in this case, O_4—roll along the lane right off O_2's cut. If he is free anywhere in this area, we feel he should be able to go to the basket in most cases. This is a free option. If he does not get the pass by the time

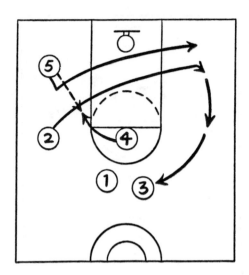

Diagram 5-3

he reaches a low post position, he would move on across the lane to the other side. From this alignment, O_5 could move to Area 4 and complete the Drop-Step Play as usual, with O_1 and O_3 completing the play.

However, there are times when O_4 might receive a pass from O_5, but may not have a good scoring opportunity. In this instance, if he has a dribble left and can make it to Area 4, he will simply go there. O_5 would cut to the basket on a backdoor or middle cut after O_4 approached Area 4. If he is not open, O_1 and O_3 would already be well-positioned to complete the play, regardless of who took it to Area 4. Diagram 5-3 shows that situation.

If the situation were reversed and the first pass went to the other side, the play would be mirrored, of course, in exactly the same way.

From a defensive standpoint, the 1-3-1 presents several different situations than a 1-2-2; while from the offensive standpoint, there is really very little which needs adjustment. Sooner or later the defense will realize that they have been hit by the same play, but since several variations have occurred in the meantime, it may be too late to make very effective adjustments. If the set is played honest, you can still go to the regular plays even if the options are stopped. If the defense decides to be complacent and waits for the completion of the play, they could easily get "burned" on the options in the meantime.

Another single-guard formation which presents its own special set of difficulties for the defense is the stack formation shown in Diagram 5-4. In fact some teams are satisfied to predicate much of their entire offense on the effectiveness of this formation in freeing the good shooter. All of

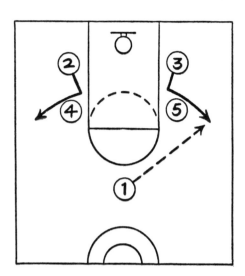

Diagram 5-4

the defensive adjustments necessary to counter-act the stack take time and effort, and even though the stack is only one of many formations in this offense, a team which wishes to prepare adequately must consider the stack in its preparation.

Though Diagram 5-4 shows a double stack, you can also run a single stack to one side or the other. Once the "bust out" occurs, however, the situation is almost identical, regardless of whether a single or double stack is used.

If O_2 and O_3 have both freed themselves, O_1 can go to either side. In Diagram 5-4, O_1 hits O_3 with the initial pass. Obviously, if O_3 were free for a good shot, he would first look for this opportunity. Assuming that this is denied, however, the offense would continue on a normal basis.

To run the Drop-Step Play, O_5 would simply move to the corner after O_3 received the pass (Diagram 5-5). You will also note that men on the side opposite the ball have reverted back to the same positions as they would occupy in the 1-2-2 formation. Therefore, once O_5 makes his move to the corner, the movement of the play is identical with the basic 1-2-2 set already shown.

On occasion, though, we have used the double stack as the springboard for a temporary 1-4 formation (Diagram 5-6) which provides us with a few additional options at no expense to the main offense.

There is really no reason why you couldn't line up in a 1-4 at the outset, except that the stack is more effective against teams which try to deny you the pass to the wings. Besides, going from a stack to a 1-4 gives the defense the problem of mentally adjusting to the special problems of

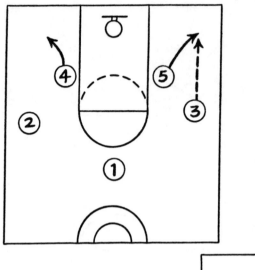

Diagram 5-5

Diagram 5-6

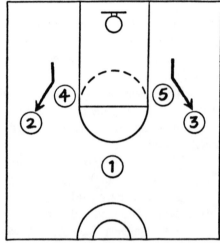

two different formations within a matter of seconds. Some teams are not up to the task.

In any event, once the 1-4 is established, and the ball is passed to either side, the movements are the same, whether a stack is used or not.

In Diagram 5-7, O_2 receives the pass from O_1. Once the pass is received, O_4 moves to Area 3 as he normally would. However, a defense which has been led to believe that this offense affords little movement on the weak side, may be in for quite a surprise. As soon as O_4 has cleared his area, leaving the middle open, O_3 makes a sharp cut off O_5 into the foul lane. If the defense switches and O_3 is not free, O_5 will then roll across the lane.

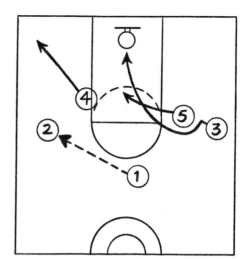

Diagram 5-7

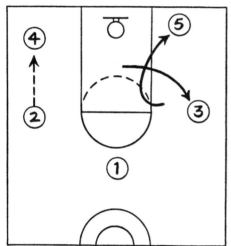

Diagram 5-8

If neither man is open, each continues on through the lane and back out to the side from which he entered (Diagram 5-8). O_2 would then hit O_4 in Area 3, and the Drop Step would continue on as usual.

In many instances, however, the play is not run to completion, as the quick cuts off the 1-4 yield many easy scoring opportunities beforehand.

The last orthodox single-guard formation which we have used on occasion is a triangle set. This formation is shown in Diagram 5-9. With the lines drawn, connecting each of the positions, it is obvious why the formation is so called. Though entire offenses are built around the possibilities of this formation, we have been most interested in a few simple cuts from the triangle. (The possibilities for a shuffle from this formation

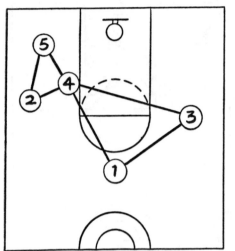

Diagram 5-9

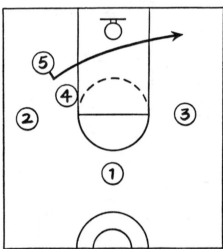

Diagram 5-10

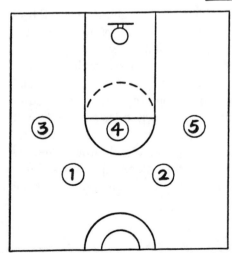

Diagram 5-11

will be dealt with in a later chapter on Blending Area Keys into your present offense.)

If O_1 decided to make his initial pass to O_2, we would run the offense much the same as with a 1-3-1 formation, with O_2 hitting O_5 and then cutting through while O_4 rolls after him.

However, if O_1 hits O_3, we put in a few more "wrinkles." As soon as O_3 receives the pass, either O_2 or O_5 will cut off of O_4 toward the foul lane. If he is free, we go for the quick pass and lay-up. If O_4's man switches on the cutter, O_4 will roll to the basket.

Though there are various ways to determine whether O_2 or O_5 should make the cut, probably the simplest key is to have O_4 turn in the direction of either man. That would make him the designated cutter.

In Diagram 5-10, O_5 makes the cut. It is assumed in this situation that he does receive the pass from O_3. In this case, he goes in through the lane and along the base line to Area 3, where he is ready to receive the pass from O_3. From this point on, the play is run as usual.

If O_2 makes the cut, the same situation would hold true for him. If there was a roll by O_4, he would execute the same move as with the 1-3-1 if he did not receive a pass; i.e., he would circle back out again.

You could also send both O_2 *and* O_5 through on cuts if you wanted to add another option. In this instance, you could merely designate the first cutter to go through to Area 3 on the ball side and have the second cutter circle back out. This would be a matter of choice. The main thing to remember is that someone must eventually move to Area 3 on the ball side in order for the play to continue.

Next we will go to the two-guard formations.

Aside from certain unorthodox formations, there are really only three basic double-guard formations, the 2-3, 2-2-1, and the 2-1-2.

Though we have seldom used the 2-3 or 2-2-1 formations, there are a few possibilities which have been discovered.

The 2-3 is usually used for a set play offense or as a free-lance set by some teams. By its very nature the 2-3 (as shown in Diagram 5-11) draws the defense outside. If you do not have a big man who is effective inside, it might be considered.

What it affords is an opportunity for the quick outside men to make the off-side cut to the basket or the wings to go 1-on-1. Whether movements are set for plays or free-lanced, they can fit into the Area Key Offense by having Area 3 covered at some point on the ball side.

However, any two-guard offense almost automatically means that

Area 1 will be by-passed, since the guards are usually set on each side of Area 1.

If O_1 were to hit O_3 there would be no problem, as the play would be keyed from that point. Once O_3 has the ball, he can first look for the 1-on-1 move. If this brings no result, someone would have to cover Area 3 to make the play work. Whenever Area 3 is not easily accessible, there is no sense in merely moving a man there without looking for a score on that move.

With the 2-3, one logical maneuver is to have O_5 make a quick flash to the basket. If nothing results, he can then move on to Area 3 and nothing is lost.

Another possibility is to have O_2 make a cut off O_4, either going over the top or behind him. O_2 could then move on to Area 3 if nothing results from the original cut.

Once the ball has moved from Area 3 to Area 4, the basic movements are shown in Diagram 5-12. O_3 hits O_2 in Area 3 and then cuts for the basket. If he does not receive a return pass, O_4 would roll off of O_3's cut as in the 1-3-1. From here the play is fairly standard, with O_2 moving to Area 4 on the dribble and O_5 moving to the top of the key with O_1 for the drop step.

If the pass to the wings is being seriously challenged, another possibility is to have the ball advanced to Area 2 on the dribble. As shown in Diagram 5-13, O_2 would "bump" O_5 out of Area 2 to Area 3. O_2 would then advance to Area 2 himself. Essentially what you have here is a situation almost identical to the 1-3-1. However, by starting in the 2-3 set, you may temporarily fool the defense by forcing them to adjust to an offensive set they seldom see.

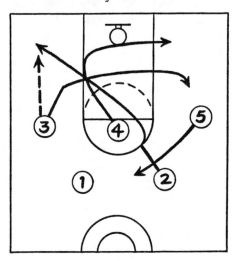

Diagram 5-12

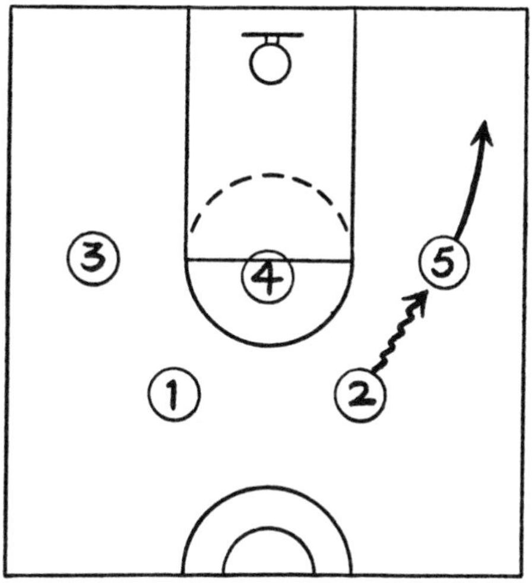

Diagram 5-13

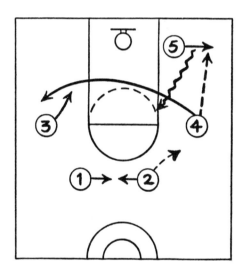

Diagram 5-14

With the 2-2-1 the workings of the play are a little more natural, since there would be a base-line man who could easily move to Area 3 once the ball has entered Area 2.

However, as with the 2-3, the ball could be advanced to Area 2 with a dribble, and the wing man on that side could move down to Area 3.

A logical sequence for the play with a 2-2-1 set is shown in Diagram 5-14. O_2 would hit O_4 in Area 2. O_4 would then pass to O_5 and move out through the middle. From here O_1 and O_2 would form "the marriage" at the top of the key, while O_5 prepares to dribble into Area 4. O_3 would move from the wing to a low post on his side.

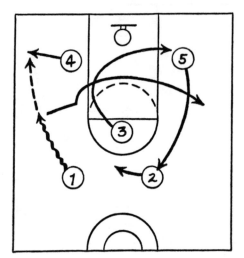

Diagram 5-15

Diagram 5-16

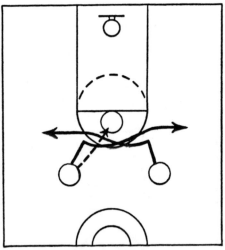

If the pass were made to the other side, there would be a natural 1-on-1 situation for O_3. As with any of the other formations, if the 1-on-1 maneuvers are not fruitful, the nearest man will then move to Area 3. In this formation it would be O_5.

The last standard formation to be discussed here is the 2-1-2, and it is one we have gone to quite often in the past.

Diagram 5-15 shows the two base-line men lined up tight. They may be spread wider depending on your plans for the high post. Spreading wider gives them more room to maneuver inside if they have good 1-on-1 moves. Using the tight alignment allows a little more maneuverability in getting free in Area 3. It also allows you to use them as low posts to be hit direct in that position. Rebounding is also enhanced by the tight formation.

The 2-1-2 in its standard version requires the ball to be advanced to Area 2 on the dribble. We often use this formation when an effective overplay on the wings denies the pass there.

As O_1 dribbles to Area 2, O_4 breaks to the corner where he receives the pass. After O_1 makes his cut, O_3 will follow on his tail as in the 1-3-1. Meanwhile, O_5 moves up to pair off with O_2 at the top of the foul circle.

However, we often like to hit O_3 direct in the high post and run a double cut off him. These movements are further extended as shown in Diagram 5-16. Naturally, if the cuts free us for the short jumper or the driving lay-up, we will take them. If neither man is open on the cuts, both swing out to the wings. From here, O_3 can hit either man on the wing. Once the ball is received on the wing, Area 3 becomes live, and the play is run in a normal fashion.

Unorthodox Formations

Though some of these movements may seem contrived in order to make the Drop-Step Play work, they're really quite logical and have usually grown out of actual game situations. Also, it should be stressed again that you may not use all of these formations regularly in a given year. To do so, however, requires much less adjustment than you might think.

This same principle applies to the temporary employment of unorthodox formations. For particular games we have occasionally gone to a totally new formation, and we have found that this can be accomplished with very little preparation.

One such formation we have employed is a two-guard out, single stack shown in Diagram 5-17. This formation has been used primarily to free the good inside man (O_4) when we might otherwise have trouble doing so. He can break to the inside or the outside for the quick shot or inside move.

Now such moves on the stack side may be fine in theory, but it they fail to produce the desired results, this formation seems ill-designed to run the regular plays or achieve a sense of continuity. This is not the case, however. If you examine the formation more closely, you will see that the side opposite the stack has all the same capabilities as the 2-1-2 set for running the Drop-Step Play.

Therefore, you can make your free-lance moves to one side and still

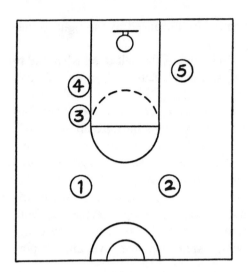

Diagram 5-17

have a normal pattern on the other side if they break down or "go dry."

At times we have also toyed with other unorthodox formations, such as various overloads to either side, triple posts (two highs and one low), an off-centered 1-3-1 (two high posts and a wing, with the guard lined head-up on the post to the side of the wing), etc. You are limited in this respect only by your imagination. The point is, with just a little more insight and imagination, you can find a relatively easy way to fit the Drop-Step Play into virtually any formation your wildest imagination can dream up without defeating any special purposes you have in mind for these formations.

In fact, I would challenge you to present a viable formation which could not incorporate the Drop-Step Play. If you feel you have such a formation and cannot work in this play without excessively contriving the situation, I would be more than happy to communicate my feelings and offer my help if you are sincerely interested. For this reason the Drop-Step Play could properly be called the Universal Play of this entire offense. It is the "bread and butter" play. The other plays, as was mentioned before, were added for "dessert." They are more specialized, and for this reason, they are not as purely adaptable to a total system of multiple formations.

Yet, I think you will see that this "lack of adaptability" is evident only by comparison with the enormous versatility of the Drop-Step Play. The other plays are also subject to multiple formations, just fewer than the Drop-Step Play.

Alternate Plays from Various Formations

As was stated in the last chapter, the first of these plays, the Scissors, was instituted to capitalize on specific defensive adjustments designed to stop the pass to Area 3. It seeks to by-pass Area 3 while hitting a man directly in Area 4. If the intent of the Scissors is analyzed, it is clear that the whole play revolves around hitting the man who would normally go to Area 3 in Area 4 instead.

What is needed to set this play up then, is a man in Area 4 and a man in Area 2 on the same side, with Area 1 occupied also. This situation can occur in several formations.

As was illustrated in Chapter 3, this situation could easily be initiated from the 1-2-2 set by having the base-line man step up to Area 4. The double stack leading to the 1-4 set will also introduce this situation if the post man holds. Both of these formations have already been illustrated in Chapter 3 (Diagrams 3-7 and 3-8). The single stack can also allow this play to occur to the side of the stack or the other side if the post man steps up as in the 1-2-2.

In all of these formations, the play is virtually identical to the way it was diagramed in Chapter 3.

It is slightly more unusual, but not necessarily contrived, to run the play from a 2-2-1 formation. In Diagram 5-18, O_2 passes to O_4. Simultaneously, O_5 will move up to Area 4. This gives you the triangle which characterizes this play. After O_4 passes to O_5, he makes the drop step from the side angle. As soon as he completes his cut, O_2 makes his move.

When you split the post in this manner, it is the second cutter who is

Diagram 5-18

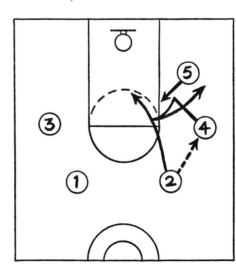

usually open. However, if the first man around is free, and it appears there is no help from the other cutter's defender, he should receive the pass. O_5 is in full view of the situation, and he must decide who will receive the pass.

This same play can be set from the 2-3 formation by moving the high post man over to the side of the lane in Area 4 instead of keeping him on the middle of the foul line. All other movements are identical.

This play is not well suited to the 1-3-1 or 2-1-2 as the high post man is too close to Area 4. Naturally, the post man could move to Area 4 as with the 2-3, but there would be another man low, moving to Area 3 on the ball side. With Areas 2 and 3 occupied and the ball in Area 4, we use the Side Drop as our primary play. To do otherwise would unnecessarily complicate the situation.

The Side Drop can be executed from almost all of the basic formations, and though not as versatile as the Drop-Step Play, it is, nonetheless, a very useful safety valve in numerous instances.

This play operates when a man in Area 4 has the ball and *both* Areas 2 and 3 are occupied. In Chapter 3, it was shown how this situation can occur as a result of a man "flashing the post" from the weak side (Diagrams 3-11 and 3-12) in a 1-2-2 formation. The flash post from the weak side can set this play up from two other basic formations as well, the 1-4 and the stack. This would occur when the ball is passed to Area 2, and the high post man on the ball side moves to Area 3 instead of holding in Area 4 as in the previous play. Once the flash post man receives the pass in Area 4, the play is run the same as with the 1-2-2 set.

Diagrams 5-19 and 5-20 show these moves from both formations,

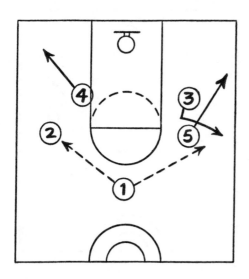

Diagram 5-19

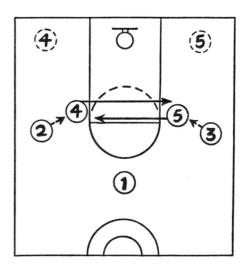

Diagram 5-20

one on each side. (Though these diagrams are meant to show both forma-tions as if they were identical on both sides, they actually portray a viable unorthodox formation from which this play can be run.) In any event, once the stack is broken by the bust-out (as on the right side), both situations are identical.

On the left side, O_4 breaks to Area 3, while O_5 flashes across the lane. On the right, O_5 goes to Area 3, as O_4 flashes across the lane. In both circumstances, the triangle is formed to set up the Side Drop.

This same triangle can be set very easily from formations using a high post by having the post man roll to Area 4 (before or after he receives the ball).

For instance, in the 1-3-1, once the pass goes to the man in Area 2, and the base-line man breaks to Area 3, the post man can roll down to Area 4 to receive the pass. Also, if the pass is thrown directly to the high post man, he can dribble to Area 4 to set up this play (Diagram 5-21).

With the two-guard formations, the high-post roll to Area 4 will be equally effective. Though it could be designed so that this play would operate from the 2-2-1, we do not employ this formation for the Side Drop. The 2-3 and 2-1-2 are well suited for this play, however.

In the 2-3 set, the Side Drop can be executed if the wing man is displaced to the corner and the guard advances the ball to Area 2 on the dribble. With a roll by the high post, the necessary triangle will be established. (See Diagram 5-22.)

With the 2-1-2 no displacement is necessary (since there is already a base-line man to cover Area 3), though the ball must still be advanced on

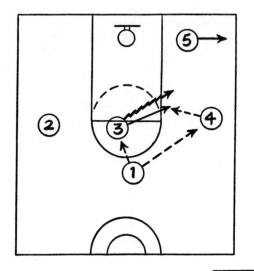

Diagram 5-21

Diagram 5-22

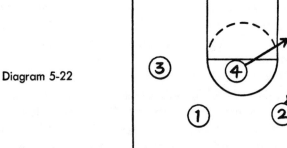

a dribble to Area 2. A roll by the high post to Area 4 will then set up the same situation as with the 2-3.

However, with the 2-1-2 we have found another way to run the Side Drop as an extension of splitting the post after the direct pass to the high post. (See Diagram 5-16.)

If this maneuver yields no results, and both cutters move on to Area 2, the high post man can then dribble to Area 4 to set up the Side Drop as shown in Diagram 5-23.

This move is a perfect example of the unpredictability of this offense from a defensive standpoint. Whereas, splitting the post can result in the regular Drop-Step Play if the post man makes an outlet pass to Area 2 and holds, by dribbling to Area 4 an entirely different play is keyed. If the defense relaxes, waiting for the movement of the ball to Areas 2, 3, and 4, they could easily "get burnt" on the Side Drop.

The one formation which requires no adjustments whatsoever is the triangle. By hitting the side to which the triangle is set, the ball simply must go into the post to run the Side Drop. This pass can be made from either the point or the wing.

Naturally, any unorthodox formation that would set up the wing-post corner triangle can be employed for the Side Drop.

The one play that is quite restricted as to the number of formations employed is the Bounce Pass Play. This is mainly because the play itself operates largely outside the principles or rules of the offense. It is also the only play which does not employ the drop-step maneuver.

The play is based on a double low pick opposite the ball with the man making the pass being one of the picks. (See Diagram 3-14.) This situation occurs most naturally from the 1-2-2 set. Obviously, you could contrive the play from many formations, but this offense thrives more on the naturalness of the moves than any artificiality of design for specific plays.

For this reason, we never run this play from any of the two-guard formations. Any formations with a high post are also unacceptable. You can't properly set a double pick for a high post because of the poor angle, and if you pick for a low post with a high post in the formation, the high post would form an obstruction. The 1-4 presents the same difficulty in terms of a poor angle as the high post sets, as does the double stack. Since the triangle presents a situation similar to a high post set, it is also a poor formation for this play.

Diagram 5-23

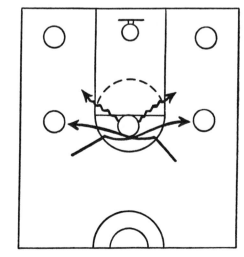

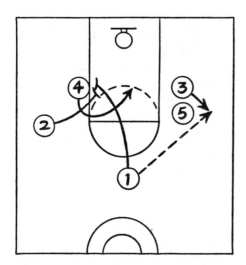

Diagram 5-24

Therefore, of our basic formations, only the 1-2-2 is really adequate. However, a slight variation from some of these other basic sets provides the same possibilities.

A single stack, for instance, gives the proper positioning opposite the stack (Diagram 5-24). Likewise, if no pressure is put on the pass to the wing (O_3), he could line up in Area 2 originally while O_5 remains in the post position. If O_5 makes the same move as on the stack, identical positioning would occur.

In general, though, this play is the most restrictive in the offense in terms of scope, but is probably the most effective of the three alternate plays. It is so much like the Drop-Step Play originally, and it is so quick to strike, that most teams are totally unprepared when it does come. It is also the only set play that strikes from the weak side. By keeping the weak side honest, many more options can be run effectively. The weak side is much less likely to cheat if definite scoring opportunities are present from that area.

Again it should be repeated that this description of the basic plays from various formations is by no means definitive. Because we don't choose to run certain plays from certain formations does not mean that you cannot do so. For us it may seem contrived to run the Bounce Pass from a 2-2-1. If this is a formation you use regularly, it may not seem so contrived for you to develop this play from that formation. The same is true with all the other plays.

Conversely, you may not use any of the formations we employ, or your positioning may be different enough on the same basic formations to present a viable working arrangement.

Once you understand the principles upon which each play is based, you'll see when the various plays will work and when they won't. Situations and opportunities we haven't even thought of will arise, and you can readily capitalize on them. It is the players themselves who often prove to be the real innovators. At least we have found this to be the case. Many of the play possibilities described here went on paper after the game, not before.

Luck was once defined as "preparation meeting opportunity." Opportunities will arise for you to incorporate unique aspects into this offense. If you are prepared when they occur, I'm sure this offense will prove as effective and reliable for you as it has been for us, while your own ideas about the use of different formations should make it just as versatile, if not more so.

6 | *Countering Defensive Adjustments*

$\mathbf{R}$egardless of how potent any offense may appear on paper or even in its initial stages of operation, you cannot count on maintaining this potency indefinitely without anticipating certain adjustments on the part of the defense. To feel your basic offensive attack is flawless in principle, and hence unbeatable, is pure folly. You are only inviting defeat by such arrogance. With the great degree of sophistication of today's defenses and the highly creative and technical abilities of today's coaches, it would be far safer to assume that certain adjustments *can* be made to hamper any offense, if not stop it.

Though some adjustments by the defense will no doubt completely surprise you and require on-the-spot counter-adjustments, many adjustments can be anticipated beforehand, and planned counter-adjustments can be worked in as a regular part of the offense.

Since your team will know the offense best, they will also know where it can be hurt the most. As explained in an earlier chapter, we have usually found our second team is our most valuable asset in this respect. If anybody can find your most vulnerable spots, it's the second unit. They know the offense, and in daily practice sessions they use this knowledge to try to stop the offense when they are on defense. We seldom discourage such attempts, as we feel it ultimately enhances our knowledge of our offensive capabilities. Eventually, the most comfortable and effective counter-adjustments are worked out in this way.

Inevitably, many of the same adjustments made by our second unit are employed by our better opponents. Consequently, we are usually quite well-prepared for these adjustments.

There is one problem with this system of anticipating adjustments, however. It has to do mainly with the physical ability of the players on your second unit. In most cases, your best athletes, physically, will comprise your starting unit. There are, therefore, certain definite limitations as to what successful adjustments can be made on a purely physical basis, especially quickness, by the second unit. However, in some cases, you will find that your opponents can make certain adjustments strictly on the basis of superior physical factors (speed, quickness, agility, jumping ability, etc.). In such instances you must know your own team's physical strengths and limitations, and anticipate the same for your opponents as much as possible. If in doubt in this respect, it is probably better to overestimate your opponent's physical abilities than to underestimate them. Unfortunately, in the past we have failed to correctly evaluate the real abilities of some of our opponents and found them making adjustments we did not anticipate. I think we have learned our lesson.

In any event it is not wise to say, "They can't do this" or "They can't do that to us." It's much safer to assume that some opponent *can* do the unthinkable and prepare for it beforehand.

The essential purpose of this chapter is to present the most common and potentially damaging adjustments we have incurred in our experience with the Area Key Offense, as well as the best means we have found to counter these adjustments.

To make any seriously threatening adjustments to this offense, two things are necessary—knowledge and time. Even assuming that your opponents have a full understanding of your offense (which is not actually plausible, for only you really understand your full capabilities), they would seldom have the time to prepare system-wide adjustments. Teams spend the greatest portion of their pre-season time preparing for the general season, not particular opponents. Once the regular season begins, most successful teams take one game at a time. This means that any opponent will seldom have more than a week to prepare for your game, and this week must be spent on all facets of the game. Unless you have a sieve defense, your opponent will have to spend a good deal of time on its own offense. The remaining time for its defense will not be enough to fully appraise team members of your total system (even if it were understood) without risking the danger of "overcoaching."

In most instances, therefore, the adjustments you will see will most likely be specific "spot" adjustments, and the major portion of this chapter will be devoted to such moves.

Overcoming Full-Court Pressure

However, there is one systematic adjustment that can be made by the defense which could seriously impair any offense if not prepared for properly. This is the full-court press.

In attacking the full-court press, we like to first ask ourselves the question, "Why are they pressing us?"

In general there are several reasons why teams press full court:

1. They may simply wish to speed up the tempo.

2. They may wish to wear an opponent down physically.

3. They may need the ball via turnovers.

4. They might try to create a psychological climate of pressure which upsets some teams.

5. They might desire to alter basic offensive patterns by forcing teams to shoot before the offense is properly set, especially if they are at a disadvantage inside for rebounding.

6. They have a poor offense and must rely on their defense to provide scoring opportunities.

Most man-for-man defensive teams will not usually employ a zone press because of the difficulty in "matching up" properly after the ball passes half-court. Therefore, what we are basically dealing with here is the full-court, man-for-man pressure defense. Of course, traps similar to zone presses may be employed by means of the double team.

In combating the man-for-man press, we have some basic principles upon which we base our style of play.

First, we decide how we can best hurt the opponent with our offense in general. As stated earlier, our facility situation dictates that we practice on a half of the court. Therefore, we operate best under these conditions. Consequently, we prefer to play most teams a half-court at a time.

This decision will obviously be affected by the situation of the game, however. If we must play "catch-up ball," we will have to look for the quicker score.

We also must compare the physical ability of ourselves and our opponents. If they are a slower but stronger team, we will obviously play them differently than a quicker but smaller team.

Lastly, we take into account the nature of the press. If it's a conservative, steady type, we will react differently than with a high-risk, gambling type press having easy openings for the score.

In any event, our primary goal is to play *our* type of game and not theirs.

To go back to the reasons why teams press, then, we can generally say that our reaction would be as follows:

If we feel they want to speed up the tempo, we will ease up the ball.

Since we seriously stress conditioning, we seldom find that an opponent can severely "wear us down" any more than they would be "worn down."

If they need the ball, we protect it that much more. This also means no easy exchanges of possession off the boards because of bad shots.

When the opponent seeks to create a climate of psychological pressure, we will seek to methodically destroy this intent by playing at as "cool" a pace as possible. If this tactic is successful, it is they who can become psychologically perturbed.

Since our basic strength is in setting up at half-court, we will not allow the opponent to force us to play a fast break type of game when we feel that is their aim.

Lastly, if they want to score, they will have to do it with their offense not their defense. Therefore, we will not play a high-risk game with a poor offensive team under any circumstances.

You must obviously be aware by now that we have little intention of going for the quick score against the press. There are numerous coaches who would argue that this philosophy is unsound, since a pressing team apparently has nothing to lose and everything to gain. I disagree.

Most coaches who argue along this line usually favor the fast break type of game and are good at it. They want to run, and a pressing team is playing into their hands. If you are not a good fast break team, why indulge in a style you are not prepared to execute effectively?

Then too, what about the idea that the defense has nothing to lose? Pressing defenses are more subject to foul trouble. Many teams cannot afford this. And what of the issue of stamina? Pressing can physically deteriorate a team while a moderate press offense is not nearly so demanding.

If you can avoid turnovers against the press, the tactical and psychological advantages you gain may easily compensate for potential risks.

In breaking the press and then setting up the regular offense at our basket, one major difficulty that must be overcome involves having the offense originate in a key area. If the ball penetrates mid-court in random fashion, before most of the team does, it could involve a confusing rush to positions or reworking the ball to a key area. Though positioning is not essential, since anyone can play anywhere, we do like certain people to play certain positions in certain situations.

Therefore, we generally get the ball to our best ball handling guard as soon as possible and have him take the ball up alone. This allows our other men to move down court and establish their normal positions, so they are ready to execute the offense as soon as the ball arrives. By clearing out and isolating the dribblers, we also minimize the chance of a successful double team and trap. If a double team is attempted, we feel the second man will be far enough away originally to give us time to react. As soon as a defender leaves one of our other men, our players are instructed to alert the ballhandler, and the man whose defender leaves moves to an open area for a pass. This man then takes the ball down court.

Since there will probably be three other men already positioned in the fore-court when he arrives, he can easily initiate a play by taking the ball to a key area. Because he is moving the ball on a dribble and is not the primary ballhandler, this area will usually be Area 2.

If his man has not yet recovered when he hits Area 3, he should receive a return pass on his cut to the basket. Of course, if none of the other remaining defenders even attempts to halt his progress when across mid-court, he could avoid the pass to Area 3 and drive right in for the short jumper or lay-up.

If for some reason, we really want to slow down the action, this man may also hold up after crossing mid-court and wait for the "isolation man" to arrive to return the ball.

In general, though, if you isolate your best ballhandler quickly and stay far enough away, most teams will find that the risks are too high in trying for the double team.

Most often, therefore, you will be able to bring the ball up 1-on-1. Ten seconds is a long time, and occasionally there is a tendency to underestimate exactly how long it is. But we have *never* had a "ten-second call" go against us, even when it appears that we are "walking" the ball up court. In fact, we have found that the biggest danger lies in being "suckered" into dashing up a sideline. Once the distance between men is cut down, the trap becomes much less risky and, therefore, much more likely, and it is also much more effective when a dribbler must halt quickly after a full-speed run. The tendency is to panic when an apparent open lane is cut off suddenly.

In essence, then, we like our ballhandler to follow a few simple principles. The first is that, to the best of his ability, he should control the speed at which he advances the ball. Secondly, we like him to stay as close to the middle of the court as possible to avoid sideline traps. Third, we do not want him to "back up court," since he cannot quickly see a double team coming, and he will be unable to spot an open man immediately if he does know it's coming. To effect a change of direction, therefore, we encourage use of the quick-spin dribble, the "through the legs" dribble, and the quick, smooth front change-of-hands maneuver. If the ballhandler can *master* it, we also allow a behind-the-back dribble. Many of these maneuvers were once considered "hot dog" moves. Today they are not only accepted but represent a tremendous advantage in that the ballhandler always has a clear view of the action in front of him.

Conditioning is essential if you have only one really adept ballhandler, since some teams will rotate assignments on this man to try to "wear him out."

A great ballhandler is worth his weight in gold in our scheme, even if this man never scores a point, for once the ball passes mid-court, and we are set up, we feel that we can inevitably free someone for the good shot. If he can score also, it's a bonus in our estimation.

Once the ball crosses mid-court against the press, there are two factors that dictate your success. The first of these is that the ball is taken to a key area in such a way that a good pass can be made to the next area when the opening occurs. (We generally want this man to take the ball to Area 1 in all one-guard formations.) The second vital element is timing. Breaks to the "live areas" must not be made too soon before a proper pass can be executed. The ballhandler must also be careful that he does not pick up his dribble too soon or too late in order to make the good pass. He must be in control at all times.

Once we are set in this manner, we feel that we have defeated the purpose of the system-wide adjustment the full-court press tries to establish. If not in total control of the situation, the offense is, at least, now able to operate more on its own terms. From this point on, most defensive adjustments will be specific and primarily individual in nature.

Hitting Area 2 Against Pressure

One of the most common spot-adjustments made by defenses which have scouted the frequency of this offense is to try to cut off the pass to Area 2. Most opponents obviously feel that if they can stop the pass to this area, they can "nip the offense in the bud."

Total denial of this pass can cramp the style of this offense, but it cannot halt it by any means. If all else fails, the pass to Area 2 can be eliminated, and the ball can be advanced on a dribble. This will be covered later. First the matter of overcoming pressure on the pass will be covered.

In this respect, several counter-adjustments can be made. Since denial to Area 2 takes the form of an overplay on the wings, you can first try to beat the defender to Area 2 by starting in tight (near the foul line) and "busting out." This move has been shown in several previous diagrams from the basic 1-2-2 formation. If the wing men are quick enough, they should be able to free themselves on the wings.

If the defense anticipates this move and cheats toward Area 2, a simple backdoor cut can prove quite effective (Diagram 6-1). With a good team defense though, the man guarding O_4 and O_5 will naturally move up to cover O_2 and O_3. However, if the pass is received by O_2 or O_3, a quick "dump" pass to O_4 or O_5 can easily result in a lay-up in this situation.

If none of these moves prove fruitful, you can easily resort to formations like the double stack to free the man going to Area 2. Many teams will play the stack from the inside and concede movement away from the middle to the wings. If the defenders line up to the outside, we will just break our low man to the middle for a quick pass. When the defender on the top switches, the offensive man on top can break to the wings. (See Diagram 6-2.)

Several teams now prefer to play the stack by having the top defender take the first man who breaks to the outside while the second man takes the inside cut. Though this move could cut off the pass to the wing initially, it could also create a mismatch. You should be alert to this possibility and be prepared to capitalize on it.

While at least one of the moves described so far usually frees Area 2 eventually, there is always the possibility that all of them could prove unsuccessful. As mentioned earlier, whenever the pass to Area 2 is totally denied, the ball can still be advanced on the dribble.

Though this is most often done from a two-guard formation, it can also be accomplished from a single-guard set. The point guard simply

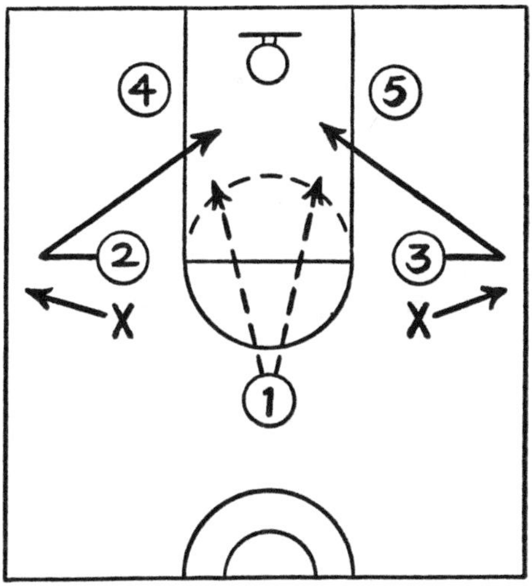

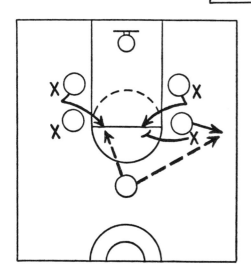

Diagram 6-1

Diagram 6-2

waves for the man in Area 2 to "clear out" and takes the ball to Area 2 himself (Diagram 6-3). If O_2 moves to Area 1 and O_3 replaces O_2, the positioning is the same as if the ball had been passed to Area 2.

However, unless there is some special necessity for running a single-guard formation, the basic two-guard fronts would most likely be used, for almost all of them naturally employ a dribble to Area 2.

Obviously, it would be ideal if Area 2 could be attacked at will, as any or all formations could be utilized as desired. Pressure and attempted denial, therefore, restrict the options available. However, there is enough variety built into the offense that the counter-adjustments described here

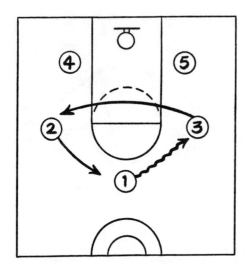

Diagram 6-3

are not deviations from the basic offense, but essential parts of it. They do not negatively affect the ultimate operation of the basic patterns.

It should also be emphasized that although we may have had to rely on several of these tactics in certain games, one or more of them always worked. We have never had Area 2 totally denied.

Adjusting to Base-Line Overplays

The next area subject to defensive adjustments is the corner or Area 3. In general, most teams usually concede lateral movement away from the basket. With the tendencies of this offense, however, some teams will try to deny the pass to Area 3 by means of a base-line overplay.

The counter-adjustments in this case are not so much systematic as individual. The base-line man usually tries to free himself by means of various cuts.

One of the most common and effective is the buttonhook. In this move the base-line man goes toward the corner at full speed. If the defender stays even or goes beyond him, he stops quickly and circles back toward the basket.

This move will not get the ball to Area 3, of course, but it does cause the defender to be quite cautious about overplays. If the base-line man does break loose, he is just about home free, as there is much less chance of help from other defenders. The only man in any type of position to help is the low weakside defender, and if he comes over, he leaves his man free on the other side of the basket. A short "dump pass" should result in

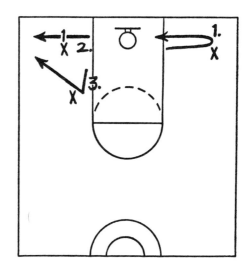

Diagram 6-4

an easy score. By using this move effectively early in the game, you may discourage any further overplays.

Another move which relies on the defensive fear of the buttonhook is a simple stop-and-go cut. Being conscious of the potential buttonhook, the defender is likely to try to recover as soon as the base-line man stops (or even slows down). Once this happens, the cutter can continue straight to Area 3.

A third move begins with a quick cut away from Area 3, toward the foul line or wing, and then a sharp break back to the corner. If the first move is overplayed, few defenders will be overly concerned about overplaying the next move down and away from the basket.

These moves are shown in Diagram 6-4.

If the individual moves fail, there are two other moves which allow the offense to continue. The first of these is a base-line pick. With this move (if there are two base-line men), the man to the ball side stays at the edge of the foul lane, and the weakside man runs his defender off the pick and continues on to Area 3 (Diagram 6-5). If a switch is effected, you are in a good position to execute a pick-and-roll.

The other counter-adjustment for overplays in Area 3 involves a complete by-pass of the area. Here the ball would merely go directly to Area 4. Ways in which this is done have already been shown.

This move will ultimately allow freer movement to Area 3, since it will take the defense's attentions away from this area. Once they become conscious of the direct hit to Area 4, they will initially be less alert about movement to the corner. Since two plays are designed for direct hits to

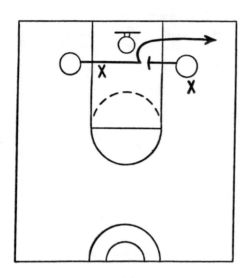

Diagram 6-5

Area 4, this move is in close harmony with the basic offense. If a team refuses to be concerned about Area 4 until the ball is in Area 3, it is just as well. Most teams are more vulnerable in Area 4 anyway.

Countering Denial to Area 4

Assuming the ball has hit Area 3, however, you must be aware of possible attempts to prevent the advance of the ball to Area 4 on the dribble. Though it is risky to overplay a dribbler going away from the basket, some teams do try it.

Two dribble maneuvers are generally used to counter-act an overplay.

If the defender is shading toward Area 4, but playing his man loosely, a simple change-of-direction dribble should accomplish the purpose. This change of direction can be done in several ways, but generally the simple cross-over dribble (front change from outside hand to inside hand) is the quickest and easiest to master, especially for the base-line men, who are not usually the best ballhandlers. If they can handle the ball well, however, a through-the-legs or behind-the-back change would certainly offer some advantages, if only for variety.

If the defender plays tight and challenges the dribble itself, we would like the dribbler to protect the ball by taking it as far to the outside as possible, even if this requires sliding up to Area 4 sideways. If the defender makes any attempt to reach in or cut off the dribble while playing tight, the dribbler drops his outside foot back toward the base

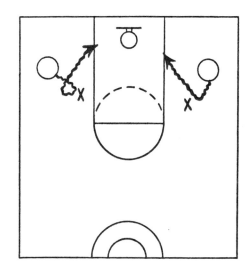

Diagram 6-6

line, hooking the defender, and simultaneously executes a spin dribble (bringing the ball around with the outside hand and changing to the other hand after spinning the body around). This move gives the offensive man inside position for the driving lay-up.

Both of these moves are shown in Diagram 6-6 (cross-over right; spin dribble left).

There is one other way in which some teams try to hamper the advance of the ball to Area 4. This is through a double team or trap on the man coming from Area 3. Under most circumstances this defensive maneuver can be "nipped in the bud," but it must be recognized quickly. Quick recognition is the key factor.

If the double team comes from the wing, the ball should merely be passed to the man from Area 2, who is making his cut after the pass to Area 3. This is shown in the right portion of Diagram 6-7.

The double team can also come from the defender in Area 1 as shown in Diagram 6-7 (left side). In this instance, either of two options can be employed. Once his man leaves him for the double team, O_1 can break for the basket. If the defender does not recover, you have a lay-up. If he does recover, the other man normally in the marriage can execute the drop step alone without O_1. The other maneuver is to have O_1 move into as close a shooting range as possible, in a position to receive a pass from O_4.

Though both of these options seem to break the basic pattern, they both yield what we consider to be satisfactory unmolested shots. Why worry about completing a play if the same net result can be achieved otherwise?

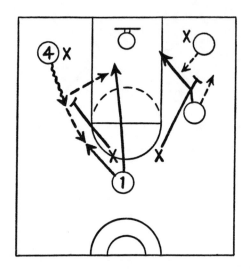

Diagram 6-7

Avoiding the Double Team in Area 4

Very closely associated with the defensive play just mentioned is the one adjustment we see perhaps more than any other—the "double team" in Area 4. A large number of teams who have seen us play on numerous occasions seem to prefer to let us advance all the way to Area 4 before they make their move. Essentially then, they play "the play."

Again, with this move, recognition is the key ingredient, especially if the defense only periodically makes this adjustment.

Once the Drop-Step Play is set (ball in Area 4 and "marriage" formed), the usual adjustment is for the defender on the inside man (closest to the ball) not to follow his man below the ball, but stay on top of the screen. He then waits there for the drop-step move to be made. Even if he does not pressure the ball, the net effect is that of a double team.

The first option in this instance is for the inside man to continue on through the lane as he does with the double team on the dribble from Area 3 (Diagram 6-8). If he does not receive the pass in the lane, he circles around the "low side" for the ball (Diagram 6-9).

If the alternate move is made, with the outside man making the drop-step move, the movement by O_1 is virtually the same (Diagram 6-10). O_3 makes the drop step, receives the pass, and gives the ball quickly to O_1 who stays low.

A second option for the double team, once the play is set, involves only a partial move by the inside man in the pair (Diagram 6-11). While

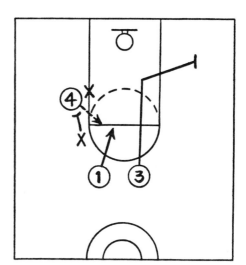

Diagram 6-8

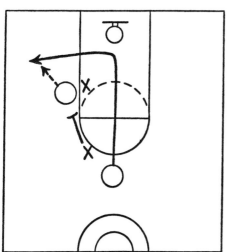

Diagram 6-9

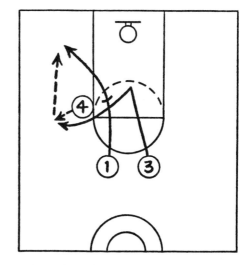

Diagram 6-10

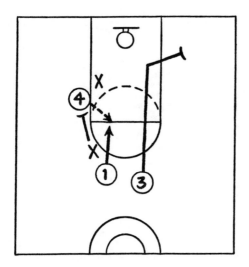

Diagram 6-11

O_3 moves down the lane as usual, O_1 stops at the foul line and waits for a pass from O_4. If O_1's man has made a serious attempt at a double team, O_1 will be open for the 15-foot jump shot, which should be desirable to almost any offense.

If the man guarding O_1 is not really commiting himself to the double team, but merely sluffing off and cheating toward the area where the drop step would be made, O_1 can execute a reverse cut (Diagram 6-12). In this maneuver, O_1 starts directly toward the outside of O_4. The man guarding O_1 would most likely counter by moving outside to get between his man and the ball. As soon as the defender starts to move to the outside, O_1 makes a sharp break back toward the key, looking for a pass from O_4. If he has a clear path for the driving lay-up, he will take it. If not, the jump shot is well within the desired range.

Most often these moves are enough to discourage a double team in Area 4. However, on occasion, a particular defender on O_1 is quick enough and smart enough to cause some considerable problems. In this instance, we don't take any unnecessary chances. If a defender is that good, we simply get him "out of our hair" early.

This is done in one of two ways. Either O_1 leaves the area early, taking the defender with him, or a formation is used where he is not likely to interfere.

By having O_1 leave Area 1 early, the drop-step move will be made by only one man. This is not unusual though, as it is done from a few formations on occasion.

Also, when O_1 leaves Area 1, the move shouldn't be made merely as

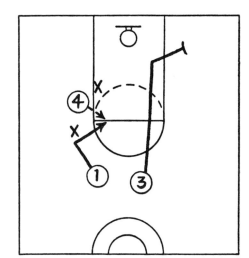

Diagram 6-12

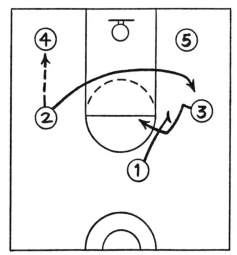

Diagram 6-13

a decoy. It can have some definite advantages. For example, in Diagram 6-13, O_4 has received a pass from O_2 and is ready to move to Area 4. At this point O_1, trying to avoid the double team in Area 4, moves toward O_3 to set a weakside pick. This move may free O_3 for an open shot or drive. If not, O_3 could continue on with the drop-step move (Diagram 6-14).

When seeking to avoid the double team in Area 4 through a change in formations, the two-guard formations are quite applicable. However, the guard controlling the ball should be the man whose defender is the one you wish to take away from the "action." Diagram 6-15 shows a 2-1-2 formation, with O_1's man the one you wish to take away from the play.

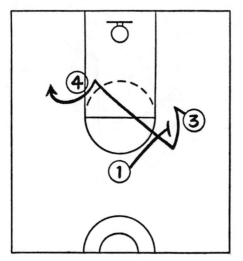

Diagram 6-14

Diagram 6-15

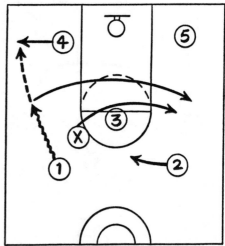

When O_1 hits Area 3 and cuts across the lane, his defender will follow. If the defender does not follow O_1, the ball should simply be reversed to O_1, who should then be free.

Other special formations or moves may be used to clear a good defender from any given area, but these are a matter of individual choice. They depend upon your own unique situation and the caliber of certain defenders at certain positions.

Though these counter-adjustments usually serve to make most teams more cautious about "playing the play," some teams will insist upon pursuing their attempts in hopes of ultimately disrupting the offense. Their probable premise is that you will be hurt eventually if forced to deviate from the basic pattern. The key point that most of them miss is that any and all adjustments you make *are* a normal part of the offense. Many of them are anticipated and prepared for in advance, while the free-lance options rest on basic fundamental moves that any well-drilled team ought to be able to execute.

Switching Formations

While most of the offensive moves described thus far center upon counter-adjustments *after* the defense has made its move, perhaps the best protection you can have against defensive adjustments is prevention.

Though many of the examples of counter-adjustments thus far seemed to involve a 1-2-2 formation, they would apply equally to several other formations as well. In fact, the best way to prevent certain adjustments is to avoid any definite overall tendencies.

If you continue to rely on a single formation to the virtual exclusion of others, you will find opponents concentrating their efforts on this formation. Therefore, when you have to utilize other formations, your execution may suffer from a lack of experience. Besides, you will probably develop individual tendencies which are difficult to break or blend into other formations.

I am not suggesting that you abandon a formation which is particularly effective in an important game. You should use what works. However, even in the "big game" a change of pace is often desirable just to prevent a breakdown in the final moments, if the defense finally learns to adjust. Even when the score is close, and no particularly damaging adjustments have yet been made, there are still times when variations are useful.

One ideal time is just after a time-out by an opponent, following an easy score by your team. The opposing coach obviously feels some adjustment must be made, whether general or specific. We feel that whatever adjusment has been made can be at least partially neutralized by temporarily avoiding the situation which prompted the move. One result is that the defenders may forget the adjustment if they are not able to use it for a few changes of possession. Another result is a psychological one. The opposing team may feel that you've "psyched them out," and/or they may doubt the wisdom of their coach in diagnosing the situation. Even if such skepticism is only temporary, you have gained an advantage.

Another ideal time to switch formations is just before the half. Prior to the half, most coaches are working out a mental picture of what has occurred thus far and what adjustments can be made. This pattern of thought can be broken by a sudden change just before the half. Even if the change is not exceptionally effective, the defense must, nevertheless, spend some time covering the implications of the new situation. That much less time can then be devoted to stopping the patterns employed for most of the game. There is also a tendency to spend a disproportionate amount of time on most recent occurrences rather than concentrate on the overall situations. For this reason, alterations made just before the half are likely to be treated with more thoroughness than they deserve.

Another opportunity you have to work on a variety of formations is against the poorer opponent. If you're definitely the superior team, there is no excuse for settling into a pattern of definite tendencies. A wide variety of formations should be employed early in the game, for once the contest has degenerated into a rout, play often becomes sloppy. This situation gives no accurate index of the true capabilities of the various formations. However, even the poorer teams will give you some indication of the effectiveness of different sets early in the game, while they still have a chance of victory.

In many cases, a team which is outmanned will either avoid a man-for-man defense altogether or switch to a zone if they find they cannot compete. In this situation, if we desire to work on our man-for-man offense we use a simple tactic. As soon as we have the lead, we hold the ball in the mid-court area until the defense is forced to come out under penalty of a technical foul. In most cases, the opponents will match up and play a man-for-man.

This tactic serves several purposes. One is that we can often score quickly because of poor reaction on match-ups. Secondly, we get to play the style of ball we want to play. Lastly, if there are any scouts present from teams which prefer to play a man-for-man defense, we demonstrate quite clearly that we have confidence in our offense and encourage the challenge.

In this last respect, some coaches would obviously disagree. Why deliberately expose your man-for-man offense to an opposing scout who plans on employing a man-for-man defense? The answer is simple. A team which basically uses such a defense will carefully scout an opponent, choosing those games where they can see what they want. If they are a worthy opponent, they will scout you on several occasions. They are, therefore, likely to see your man-for-man offense anyway. If you carefully avoid definite tendencies, especially in the "easy" games, you will present the scouts with either an unintelligible offense or one of such apparent complexity that they still may know little more of what to expect than if they didn't scout at all. If they mistakenly chart a tendency and prepare accordingly, they may be extremely vulnerable elsewhere. In essence, we feel that the possibility of having to expect almost anything is no better than not knowing what to expect at all.

However, in the intensity of a contest, it is entirely possible that a definite tendency is displayed and goes unnoticed at the time. Also, substitutions in a given game may necessitate certain limitations on varying formations. The important thing is that each game be analyzed in retrospect, either through films or charts. Once the tendency is spotted, and being fairly confident that a competent scout has also found it, you should plan your next contest accordingly. If you scrupulously avoid this tendency again or disguise it by altering your pattern somewhat, the situation may actually work to your advantage.

With the potential variety present in this offense, the opponents only think they know what to expect. They can never be sure.

Varying Plays Regularly

While varying formations is essential to maintain the flexibility of the offense, it is also necessary to use a variety of play possibilities as well.

While it is entirely too contrived to decide in advance to run all of the basic plays in some type of prescribed sequence, there are often enough situations which present themselves naturally that most of the play possibilities can be explored.

The advantages of varying the plays are virtually the same as varying the formations from the standpoints of experience, general offensive effectiveness, and difficulty of scouting.

When the two are used in conjunction (variety of formations and plays), the advantages are compounded.

However, the ultimate effectiveness of the offense occurs when the individual *options* are wisely utilized.

Use of Planned Options and Free-Lancing

The built-in options to each play rely so much on basic offensive maneuvers that it's very difficult to determine whether you're using a standard set of plays or free-lancing. From the standpoint of defensive adjustments, they become very difficult to design if the opponent is really not sure of a pattern. False "patterns" may appear merely because you find a particular weakness and exploit it regularly in the same fashion.

For example, our flashing post maneuver from the weak side is a free-lance option. However, we have found that after our regular patterned movements take effect, certain overadjustments by the defense make this move very effective. Therefore, we have capitalized on the weakness by flashing the post whenever the opportunity arises. If it is ten or even 20 times a game that the situation arises, we will use this maneuver. To the opposing coach or a scout, it may appear that this is a set play since it usually seems to occur in the same manner, preceded by the same moves, when, in fact, it is the defense which sets up this option. For the defense to readjust and cut off this option, would not affect the total offense one iota.

On the other hand, we may use certain planned options so infrequently that the defense may feel it has been victimized by a free-lance maneuver.

Because this offense allows you to operate equally well on patterned plays or individual moves, it is often difficult for opponents to tell which you are primarily relying on in any given game. Before meaningful adjustments can be made, the situation must first be accurately diagnosed. Just as an opposing coach thinks he has your system figured out, a quick-striking option can cause a whole new evaluation. Doing the unexpected can go a long way in making any team cautious about defensive adjustments.

If, and when, a team does make them, however, your own ability to diagnose the adjustments will determine your ultimate effectiveness. Even a "wrong" adjustment based on false premises can upset an offense if no sensible counter-moves are employed. It's not enough to sit back complacently and think, "They can't stop this offense." It's much more difficult, but much more effective, to sit up and determine why they won't stop this offense. The means for countering the defense are not only present in this offense, they are an essential part of it. They should be learned as thoroughly as the basic plays themselves.

Self-adjustments are possible only if you and your team are prepared to implement them.

Blending Area Keys into Your Present Offense

Dangers of All-or-Nothing Commitments

It's quite possible that the central idea of the Area Key Offense appeals to you, but you might still prefer to retain some of the offensive maneuvers your teams have found successful in the past.

Abandoning everything you've previously worked with offensively is no small decision, and many coaches are not prepared to go quite that far, at least not initially.

In fact, what turns off many coaches about the idea of adopting another offensive system is that it may require this total abandonment of all previously used plays and formations, leaving nothing to fall back on if the new system doesn't live up to its advance billings. Some offenses are so "bulky" in content that they leave little room for anything else. Others may require such a total commitment of a team's time, energy, and resources to be implemented, that there's no going back once the commitment is made.

I found this "all or nothing" philosophy associated with many offenses I was exposed to at camps and clinics I attended or in books and articles I've read. For this reason, I seldom greeted new offenses with any great enthusiasm. Most of them simply required more than I felt we were prepared to give.

Area Keys and Your Present Offense

I sincerely believe this is not the case with the Area Key Offense. The fundamental principles upon which it operates are simple to understand and implement. The basic play (the Drop Step) can be mastered with equal facility. Perhaps most important of all in terms of adjustment, the free-lance moves are those commonly used by most teams that rely on sound fundamental basketball. The emphasis placed on certain moves may differ, but the maneuvers themselves are quite standard.

It's possible that what you're really looking for is a change-of-pace offense to supplement your present one. If this is the case, the Area Key Offense could be your answer. It could be installed for a particular game with much less preparation than other offenses require. It could also fit into your regular season practice schedule for intermittent use from game to game without undue interference with your basic offense.

If your present offense, though normally effective, has been stymied by a particular team, you may want to present that team with something quite different. At least a basically operative portion of this offense could be installed in a short time. This might be that "something different" you're considering.

Or, within a given game your offense may go sour, and you may want to vary your style. Portions of this offense may be helpful here also.

However, the relationship of the Area Key Offense to your present system goes far beyond a mere supplement. In many cases it can be implemented as an integral part of your present offense.

The various offenses that follow are not a definitive list of all the possibilities for blending in the Area Key Offense. They are examples of some of the more familiar types with which you are probably acquainted.

Fast Break Offenses

Many teams predicate the bulk of their offensive success on their ability to score the fast break basket. A team which has mastered this style of play can be explosive. However, trouble often occurs when the good shot is not immediately available on the break, and the offense is forced to do one of two things—take the first shot available or stop and set up an offensive pattern.

Few coaches have the shooters necessary to play a wide-open "run and gun" game with its added difficulties of poor rebounding position.

Setting up a pattern appears to be the best option for most teams. But this too can present its own set of problems. Often the players are out of their normal positions and must reset before working the ball. Fast break basketball as a steady diet creates a frame of mind in the players that is not always conducive to the patience necessary to stop and realign.

With the Area Key Offense, a great deal of realigning shouldn't be necessary to begin operating the plays. Since positions are often interchangeable, anyone near a live area can move in it. Naturally, your players won't always be in the ideal position you'd like. But then, if the fast break fails, and you begin another series of moves immediately, the defense is likely to be out of position also. Mismatches may make up for the inadequacies of positioning in many cases. The defenders won't have any time to hunt for the "right man" to guard. They'll have to take the nearest man if there's little or no break in the action for resetting on a large scale.

For example, if the lanes are filled properly, as shown in Diagram 7-1, but the defense has recovered quickly, the break might end with O_3 having the ball in Area 2. He cannot penetrate any further, and the trailer (O_4) is also covered. O_4 can then move to the base line, and, realizing he

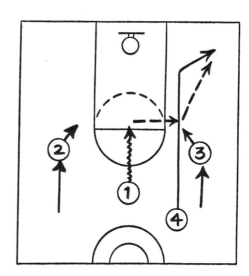

Diagram 7-1

won't receive the pass, go to Area 3 immediately. A pass from O_3 to O_4 might be a standard move even in a "run and gun" offense, and, if O_3 is a good base-line shooter, a shot by O_4 would be a feasible option. But what if O_4 is not a good base-line shooter, or he isn't open for the shot? If this offense is used as an extension of the fast break, O_4 can merely follow through with the Drop-Step Play. O_3 would make his cut after the pass, and O_1 would step back from the foul line to Area 1. O_5 would fill in the side opposite the ball.

Another play possibility occurs with an alternate move by O_4 (Diagram 7-2). Instead of moving to Area 3, O_4 executes a buttonhook cut back toward the ball. A pass to O_4 in this position sets up the Scissors Play quite easily.

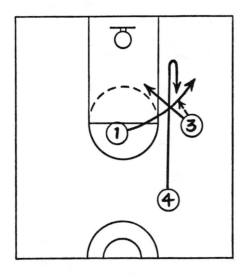

Diagram 7-2

Without going through all of the play possibilities, this should give you some idea of how the fast break need not "hang in mid-air" if unsuccessful. Immediate follow-up can ensue.

Even if the lanes aren't filled properly, someone should always be near enough to a key area for the offense to begin operating. Wherever the ball is after the break ends simply becomes a starting point for the half-court offense to begin. Though individuals may be out of their ideal positions, the offense itself is always close to being positioned properly for a play. The formations you arrive at should be no different than the ones you'd be used to if normally operating under multiple formations.

Such patterned continuity is rare in most fast break offenses, and the possibilities are worth considering if your present offense lacks it.

The Weave

The weave in one of its various forms has been employed for quite some time and by many coaches. Though today's pressure defenses, with the jump switch, double team, and attempts to draw the offensive foul have made the exchange of the ball much more difficult, the weave, or some variation of it, is still being used.

If you employ a weave as a normal offense, you may eventually be setting opponents up for a mismatch after a switch, a pick off a post-man, isolations, or backdoor cuts. Your opponents will no doubt be guarding against the same maneuvers. What they won't expect is an almost unnoticeable movement from the weave into an entirely different offense.

Whether you're using a three-, four-, or five-man weave you should have little difficulty blending in the Area Key Offense.

Since weaves concentrate on ball movement around the perimeters, the ball will almost always be in, or quite near, Areas 1 or 2. Therefore, the Drop-Step Play can easily be initiated at any time.

In Diagram 7-3, O_1, who would normally pass the ball to O_3, by-passes this exchange and dribbles to the wing. If O_5 steps out to Area 3, the elements of the Drop-Step Play are present. From this spot, the play can be run as it would be from any other 1-3-1 formation.

Just as this play can be run from almost any set formation, it can be

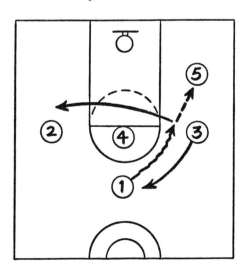

Diagram 7-3

initiated from virtually any formation used for execution of the weave.

While the play in combination with the regular weave offers some unexpected options, it should not interfere in any way with the normal operation of the weave patterns. It's simply an off-shoot of these patterns.

Triangle-Shuffle Patterns

Several years ago, before the Area Key Offense was fully developed, we occasionally used a shuffle offense from a triangle set. (This formation was already touched upon in Chapter 5.)

Certainly all "shuffles" aren't run from triangle sets, and all triangle offenses don't involve a shuffle pattern. However, I am using this rather limited example, in itself, to show that the Area Key Offense can fit into both triangle and shuffle offenses or a combination of both. Also, we are familiar through experience with the manner in which this offense can be extended.

With a normal shuffle pattern from the triangle in Diagram 7-4, O_1 would pass to O_3, and O_2 and O_5 would break off O_4's stationary pick. If neither receives the ball, O_4 would then roll across the lane. As the pattern shifts to the ball side, O_1 goes to the wing opposite the ball. If none of the cutters are open, O_3 dribbles out front and hits O_1. The same movement then continues back the other way.

These cuts may be made back and forth many times before any openings result. Just as the defense becomes conditioned to the move-

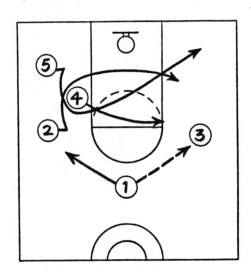

Diagram 7-4

ments of the shuffle, these movements can suddenly be set in a new direction without any break in the action.

If the first cutter in the series goes to Area 3 and receives a pass there from Area 2, "the play" is set in motion (Diagram 7-5). No key need be given other than the pass to Area 3.

Even if a shuffle isn't employed, these same types of cuts can be made from any triangle formation and extended in the same manner.

Though the shuffle gives continuity, many triangle patterns lack it. Blending in the Drop-Step Play can make basic cuts a starting point for a whole new series of moves if the cuts themselves fail to produce any scoring opportunities. Such an addition can take much of the risk out of potentially "dead end" moves from the triangle formation.

Diagram 7-5

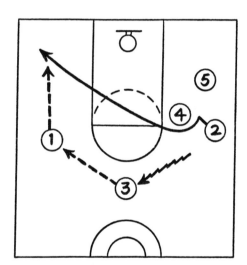

The Stack Offense

It's difficult to go through a regular season's schedule nowadays without facing at least a few opponents who employ some variety of a stack offense. Stacks come in all forms—single and double, high and low, vertical and horizontal.

Though some teams who use a stack have evolved an elaborate series of moves after the initial break from the stack, quite a few teams still rely on the stack itself to provide the opening for the shot. It is this latter situation to which I will apply my comments.

If anything, a well-designed and well-executed stack of this nature is quick striking. While normally an advantage, some coaches who use this offense will confess that it sometimes strikes *too quickly*. Not only is the defense caught a step behind, but the offense itself is occasionally unprepared to take full advantage of the opportunities present.

The stack is often broken before the ballhandler can deliver the pass, since perfect timing is difficult to achieve when moves are developed around split-second openings. Also, the potential availability of the immediate shot off the stack makes some players unable or unwilling to notice openings which may occur elsewhere. Finally, a team which is proficient at the quick strike from the stack often finds it difficult to slow down the tempo when necessary.

Some coaches feel they must accept these disadvantages of the stack as a necessary sacrifice to obtain the quick-striking capabilities.

By blending the Area Key Offense into the stack, these disadvantages can be minimized considerably, while the advantages can be maintained intact. If the quick shot is available, it can and should be taken. However, if it's denied, a whole series of contingent moves can be employed which are capable of yielding an equally satisfactory shot.

While the Bounce Pass Play is not desirable with the stack in most cases, you should be able to run the other three plays without any great contrivance.

The play possibilities from the single and double stacks parallel to the foul lane are described in Chapter 5. (See Diagrams 5-4, 5-5, 5-6, 5-7, 5-8, 5-17, 5-19, and 5-20 in Chapter 5.) These are the most common forms of the stack used. If you employ some different variations of the stack, I'm sure these too could easily be extended to include the broad range of options presented in this book.

Spot Plays

I don't think there's a basketball coach alive who hasn't seen, heard, or read about some particular play which someone else purports to be a "sure thing." It's also likely that almost all of us have yielded to the temptation to sit down at the drawing board and play X and 0 in order to come up with that "sure thing" ourselves. In fact, many of us probably have a file full of sure things, but that's where most of them stay!

What keeps us from using them? Well, for one thing, we usually try a few of them out in practice periodically, and the players screw them up so bad the first time, we're usually too embarrassed to even give them a second try. Maybe next year! There just isn't enough time to keep working at these pet projects anyway.

Occasionally, however, one of these plays clicks immediately. But still we're generally afraid to try it in a game. Why? Because quite often this play is staged from formations or patterns which differ from the usual. Also, we're afraid that, if it fails, we'll be hung up on the roof with the ladder kicked out. Where do we go from there?

Despite all the derision usually cast on these "sure things," it's unfortunate that many of them probably can yield 2 points, but aren't tried in games. An almost sure 2 points are hard to come by, and it's a shame to waste such a play if you feel you have one.

Though some coaches feel the last shot of the game is a good time, since there's no need to worry about follow-up moves, I personally feel that, except in rare instances, I'd rather go to something with which the players are really familiar. If you need that last shot to win or tie the game, the pressure is often enormous. Familiarity is usually the best cure for that.

However, the last shot of an earlier period might be a good time to try the spot play.

Another ideal chance is after a time-out, or the break between periods, when you have ample opportunity to communicate your wishes and set up the assignments accurately.

This offense can help overcome some of the misgivings about using the spot play.

Abnormal formations used for the spot play are no real problem with this offense, since players are used to operating from a wide variety of sets. One more set is not hard to accept.

As for the worry about the spot play coming to a dead end, this too should present little difficulty. If the play fails, the ball will always be near enough to a key area to continue with the basic offense. Counter-moves are built right into any play designed.

I could probably show the feasibility of adapting any play to this offense, but the number of possibilities are limited only by your imagination. You should be familiar enough with the operation of the offense by now to see how any particular play could fit into the total system.

Set Play Offenses

Closely connected to the idea of spot plays is the offensive system built around a series of set plays. While the spot plays are used only in special situations, the set play offense is actually a conglomeration of spot plays used throughout the contest. The number may vary, depending upon the ability of the players to understand the various assignments.

Set plays might be geared to setting up one key move, or they may involve a series of potential scoring opportunities. In this latter type, there is a limited degree of continuity from one move to the next. However, unlike a true continuity offense, there is a definite end to the plays eventually. Once this end is reached, there are usually no alternatives except to free-lance or stop and reset so another play can be called.

Free-lancing is fine, but it usually produces better results when you can do something else. When it comes at the end of a play, it's almost forced on you, and you may be confined to it. Also, with many different set plays in the offense, there are likely to be so many possibilities at the end of the various plays that it's difficult to plan or practice free-lance moves. After all, the term free-lance really means spontaneous, not un-prepared for.

Though we use a considerable number of free-lance moves, most of them fall within a fairly predictable range, from our standpoint at least. (Free-lance offenses were not considered here, since the following chapter deals extensively with the use of free-lance options as a standard part of our offense.)

Resetting can also be a problem, since a massive amount of reposi-tioning can be risky. You don't really expect the defense to just lie back and let you set up for a new play without challenging the ball? Once it's clear you're not looking for the score, the defense has little to lose by hounding the ball in the meantime. Also, if any defenders have left themselves temporarily vulnerable, they too have time to recover.

Some of this difficulty can be eliminated by extending the various set plays to include some elements of the Area Key Offense. With a number of set plays already in the offense, I wouldn't recommend adding too many more. However, I do think one more play could be handled. The Drop-Step, being the most universal of the four, would obviously be the best choice.

Whatever position you end up in, following the unsuccessful com-pletion of a set play, you can switch rather easily into the movements of the Drop-Step Play.

By keeping *constant* pressure on the defenders during each posses-sion, they're much more likely to commit that vital error which leads to a score, with little chance to recover.

Using Your Imagination

As I said earlier, this list of offenses is by no means a complete account of the numerous methods of attack being employed. By this time, though, I'm quite sure you can see how almost any offense can be extended beyond its normal range of operation. If you do see some value in extending your present offense, I think that with a little of your own imagination you can find a viable way to blend in some elements of this offense.

You obviously know your own offense and the offensive capabilities of your players. By this time you should also understand much of the potential of using area keys and the various plays in this offense. There's surely some way these three factors can be combined to produce a more effective attack.

If your offense is riding in high gear, you probably won't need to concern yourself about such alternatives. But, as I said before, if this were the case, you probably wouldn't be reading this book.

The suggestions presented here are meant more to stimulate your own imagination than to offer specific alternatives. Some possibilities for extension are given, but the exact form they'll take should depend upon your own ideas based on the needs and abilities of your team.

In making your decision, you should bear one important point in mind. You can use as much or as little of this offense as you need. In no case must you make a total or irrevocable commitment. The time allotted to achieve the necessary blend will depend upon the extent to which you use this offense. But in no instance should it require so much time that the execution of your present offense would suffer.

8 | *Free-Lancing with Structure (Basic Individual Options)*

Problems of Free-Lance Offense

After watching a game in which classy professionals smoothly execute a number of effective free-lance maneuvers, there is a tendency to sometimes feel that this is how the game should really be played. All of the practice time spent on perfecting set plays and patterned offenses seems so contrived and so unnecessary that many of us must often wonder why we even bother. It would be so much easier to just "let the guys play" and capitalize on situations as they occur. At least this is how it would appear.

However, on closer examination, it becomes clearer that free-lancing is not quite so easy or effective as it might seem on the surface. This is especially true in dealing with the average scholastic and collegiate athletes. There are certain problems inherent in free-lance offenses, and they should be explored openly and honestly before deciding to adopt a total free-lance system. Some of these shall be dealt with now.

On occasion I have heard some coaches lament that they have difficulty in implementing a patterned offense because their players seem to lack the sense of discipline necessary to operate this style of offense. They see a free-lance system as their only salvation. What they fail to realize is that their main problem still is, and still will be, a lack of discipline, and free-lancing is no cure for this problem. If a team is undisciplined in a patterned situation, it may very likely be worse under free-lance conditions, as almost all external controls are eliminated.

Free-lancing with the undisciplined player can, therefore, lead to several complications. One of the primary problems is the bad shot. This can manifest itself in several ways. The bad shot may be one that is taken from a range beyond which the player is reasonably accurate. It may be a 30-foot shot from a guard, or a 15-foot shot from a close-range inside man. It may merely be an off-balance shot, where the shooter is not set. Any shot under closely guarded conditions, regardless of range or balance, may be considered a bad shot. Bad shots may also be considered from the standpoint of a lack of sufficient rebounders. The undisciplined player may fire up a shot without any regard to the possibilities that he may miss and no one will be there to rebound. Finally, the bad shot may simply be a matter of bad timing. I'm sure most of us have won a game or two because an opposing player took a shot and missed when he should have held onto the ball and run out the clock or created a desperate situation for the defense.

The bad shot is not confined to the free-lance system, but the lack of control and pattern makes it even more vulnerable to this problem. With the undisciplined player, the problem is compounded.

Another major difficulty which free-lance offenses often encounter is that of monopolizing the ball. While there is little place for "ball hogging" in a patterned offense, the free-lance offense leaves more than ample opportunity to overmaneuver. In some cases, the only salvation has been the time limit imposed on dribbling in the forecourt.

"Ball hogging" can be extremely disruptive from both a psychological and a technical standpoint. Psychologically it can alienate the other members of the team and build up resentment against the "ball hog." Unless the player is a real superstar, whose excessive ballhandling has been the decisive factor in winning some really crucial games, the other players may deeply resent being left out of the game. When the time comes for others to carry the burden, they may be unwilling or even unprepared to do so.

There was once a story about a rather well-publicized Yankee third baseman who was pictured as being the backbone of the team. He was described as always "knowing what to do with the ball." With the bases loaded in the ninth inning of a crucial game, a ground ball was hit between third base and the mound. The pitcher reached it first, fielded it, and calmly handed the ball to the third baseman, saying "Here, you know what the hell to do with it." A run was scored, but the point was made.

Technically, "ball hogging" has other implications as well. First of all, the rebounders are often uncertain as to when the shot may be taken and are, therefore, out of position for the rebound in many cases. Also, while the "ball hog" is "doing his thing," the other players may be standing around not knowing what to expect. When player movement stops, most offenses stop.

However, even without the "ball hog," standing around can still present a problem in free-lance offenses. It's a common flaw. Since at any given moment a great variety of moves are possible, some players are overwhelmed by the choice and simply do nothing. They may freeze, partly out of an uncertainty as to what the other players may do at the time. While everyone is waiting for someone else to maneuver, no one does anything. There is either no particular key or too many general ones.

This situation is often corrected with an experienced, self-confident team. However, most high school and many college players lack the necessary experience to overcome the general sense of insecurity that can result from free-lancing. And don't forget, scholastic and collegiate athletes only play together for a few years, if that. Usually the team changes considerably in composition each year. Without structure or the ability to anticipate another's moves, each maneuver can seem like an experiment, and most players are afraid to experiment when the outcome of the various moves is so unpredictable. What if the maneuver fails? What's the next move? And the next? There is no sense of true continuity, either individually or in the total system.

These negative psychological implications of free-lancing can be as disruptive as the technical problems, perhaps even more so. It can have a carry-over effect. A normally aggressive rebounder may "back off" even slightly if he transfers the unpredictability of general offensive movement to rebounding situations. A player who becomes afraid to experiment on offense may not wish to take an occasional necessary gamble on defense. An unrestrained, undisciplined player on offense may become uncooperative and possibly foul-prone on defense. Team psychology and personality are no small matters to consider in your total scheme.

Advantages of Free-Lancing

Hopefully, it will be shown later in this chapter how the Area Key Offense can alleviate some of these strains placed on a total free-lance offense, if not eliminate many of them completely. Before doing so, however, it should be pointed out that free-lancing does present some definite advantages over totally patterned offenses.

For one thing, the positive effects of spontaneity have to be considered. Many set play offenses have to go through a series of definite prescribed moves before a particular play will take effect. Since the ultimate goal is setting up the final move for the shot, many defensive mistakes on the preliminary moves may be overlooked entirely, or there may be no freedom to take advantage of them when they occur. A lazy defensive play may go unnoticed; a foolish defensive gamble may be employed without any counter-attack. A free-lance offense is ready to capitalize spontaneously on any such defensive lapses.

Since the moves in a free-lance offense are not pre-determined, it is quite unpredictable and may strike anywhere, anytime. This not only makes on-the-spot, systematic adjustments next to impossible for the defense, but also it makes a team very difficult to scout and prepare for in advance.

In addition, a free-lance offense can capitalize on particularly weak defenders better than patterned offenses. You can "1-on-1" a weak defender to death, since he can be isolated or "set up" at will. A set play offense may not allow the proper man to be exploited as often.

There is definitely an argument to be made, therefore, for using free-lance moves. However, some of the ills present in this type of play must be overcome.

Free-Lancing with Area Keys

It has been our experience that the Area Key Offense can offer most of the advantages of a free-lance offense without most of the usual drawbacks mentioned earlier.

The possibilities of a bad shot are lessened since the Area Key Offense contains within its principles the notion of what the ideal shot would be. Any individual move must, therefore, yield as good or a better shot, or it is inherently discouraged.

The dangers of "ball hogging" are reduced, since this offense does not rely primarily on individual prowess for its success. It's a team offense, and no one individual should have that much opportunity to control the ball excessively, unless particular game conditions warrant it. Such a situation is rare, but the opportunity for individual exploitation is present, if needed. It does not become habitual though.

Lack of player movement should be no problem either, since basic movements are prescribed, regardless of what individual maneuvers are occurring. There is also a sense of predictability involved, as most free-lance moves still occur within the context of the basic plays.

This situation takes most of the risk out of experimenting. Other players' moves can be anticipated much easier, and if an option fails, there's enough continuity to dictate follow-up moves.

Perhaps most important of all, the placement of free-lance maneuvers within the context of a structured offense gives a team the sense of security necessary to operate in an aggressive, self-confident manner.

The part played by free-lancing in the Area Key Offense is an important one, but it should be emphasized that it's still only a *part* of the offense. With this in mind, I will now explain some of the basic free-lance options that can be employed.

1-on-1 Moves and Plays

The first of these involves the use of basic 1-on-1 maneuvers. In Chapter 4 the universal fakes and drives were already discussed, as they are a vital part of any team's ability to succeed in 1-on-1 situations. All of our players are schooled in the techniques for executing these fakes and drives.

However, there are some additional individual moves we like to develop, especially on the part of our inside men. They are moves to be employed close to the basket, since it's one of our primary objectives to operate for the shot as close to the basket as possible.

The first moves we work on are those designed to free a man to receive a pass in close. The chapter on counter-adjustments dealt with freeing men in the basic areas. Some of these same moves can be used to free a man in the foul lane or near it. The buttonhook, go-stop-go, and V cuts shown in Diagrams 6-4 through 6-6 are all useful for this purpose.

Diagram 8-1 shows a high post man swinging away from the ball and then buttonhooking back toward the ball. This move is most effective when the defender does not play between the cutter and the ball, but

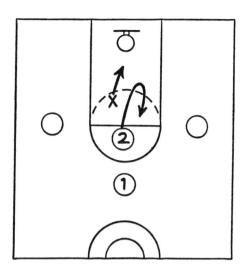

Diagram 8-1

rather stays alongside or retreats behind the cutter. With the defender to the side or slightly behind, O_2 plants his foot nearest to X, spins on the pivot foot, and comes back to meet the pass. By doing this, he can shield X from the ball with his body.

Diagram 8-2 shows O_2 moving across the lane quickly. He suddenly stops, and if the defender stops with him, gives a quick burst toward the ball. This move works best if the defender is crowding the cutter, since he

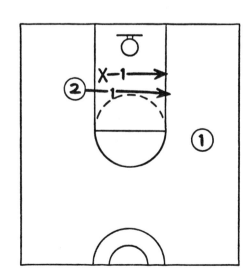

Diagram 8-2

cannot recover as fast as the cutter who knows what he's doing. After this has worked a few times, O_2 can simply flash at full speed all the way, as X is "set up" and may expect a slowdown.

The V-cut in Diagram 8-3 works best when the defender is very conscious of an overplay and fights to establish position in the high post. If this happens, O_2 plants his foot closest to the foul line and pushes off toward the base line. If the defender concedes the high post, O_2 would take it, and nothing is lost.

Another efficient move involves a hooking of the defender and a roll

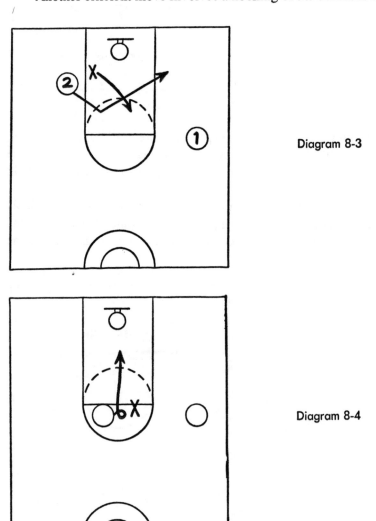

Diagram 8-3

Diagram 8-4

to the basket. In Diagram 8-4, O_2 makes a move from a high post toward the ball. If X tries to overplay and deny position, O_2 places his inside foot (left foot here) right next to the defender, with his body making slight contact. He then rolls off his pivot foot, temporarily turning his back to the ball, hooks the defender with his outside elbow and leg, and goes to the basket. If this move is executed quickly and properly, the defender should be left "on top" of the cutter. A good lead pass should set O_2 free for a lay-up.

In certain situations, when the defender stays close, this same move can be executed on a full-speed cut. Caution must be taken, however, not to make the body contact too severe, as many officials would call an offensive foul. It should also be noted that the elbow is used for hooking the man, not the arm, as this often results in what appears to be a definite hold by the offensive man. If the offensive man does not hit the defender with the point of the elbow, and he releases quickly, a foul will very seldom be called.

On occasion we have found it advisable to just allow the good big man to establish himself in a low post to the ball side. If the defense concedes the low post pass we're satisfied. In most cases, though, the defender tries to "front" or play above the low post. In this instance, our post man starts toward the ball, stops, and rolls back toward the basket. A lob pass usually gets the ball to the low post man. This move must be worked on regularly, though, as it depends largely on the timing and accuracy of the pass.

There are obviously many other cuts and moves that can be used to free your players inside. The more experienced a player becomes the more moves he can handle. For most players, however, the cuts described above should be more than enough to refine and perfect.

However, getting the ball in close is one thing; scoring is yet another. Though the standard fakes and drives can be used from 10 to 15 feet out, we try to perfect a few other basic moves for the really close shot.

It has been our experience that just as each player has his own peculiar way of shooting a jump shot, our inside men have developed one or two moves suited particularly to each of them. These might be a sweeping hook shot with no fake, an underhand "scoop shot" following a head fake, a quick pivot and a fade-away jump shot, etc. As long as they are successful we seldom interfere with these personal moves.

Nevertheless, there are a few standard maneuvers we like our inside men to master.

One of the primary moves is a "hook step." This move is used when the defender is in back of the offensive man or slightly to one side, while the offensive man has his back to the basket.

The execution of this move is very similar to the "hook and roll" described earlier, except the offensive man already has the ball. Care must be taken not to move the feet in making the first move. This first move consists of a body fake in which the head, shoulders, and ball turn to one side. The defender should try to stop this roll to the basket. At this point the foot opposite the movement of the ball is dropped back below the feet of the defender, and the body weight and direction is quickly shifted to that foot. The elbow to the side of the pivot is swung around, bringing the head and shoulders between the defender and the basket. As soon as the pivot is completed, the way is clear for a drive to the basket.

To make this move effective, both feet must be stationary when the ball is received. Then the move can be made to either side. (If the defender shades one side, the fake should naturally be made to that side.) Also the first step must be long enough to "hook" the defender.

Another effective move with the back to the basket involves a quick turnaround toward the side of the shooter's strong hand. Assuming a right-handed shooter gets the ball in the post area, he would make a quick turn toward his right side. As he is turning, he brings the ball up for a jump fake as if he is going for the jump shot. At this close range, the fake must be respected. As soon as the defensive man reacts, the ball is brought down low across the body, and a drive for the basket is made to the right side.

This move relies on quickness of execution. Also, care must be taken not to pick up the pivot foot before the ball is put on the floor for the drive.

Naturally, there are times when the good inside man can simply power his way right to the basket. When our men are this close, we prefer that they shoot a power lay-up, using the backboard. With this move, the shot is taken with the "strong hand," regardless of the side from which the shot is taken. The ball is held high and away from the defender to protect it, and the jump is made off both feet. On the jump, the body is projected towards the basket. We want a 3-point play here, not just a foul.

The Clear-Out

Though many of the 1-on-1 moves are executed spontaneously when the situations arise, there are times when you may want to deliberately create such situations. You may wish to exploit a particularly weak defender, utilize the talent of a great offensive player, or capitalize on an opponent in foul trouble (or get him in such trouble). Whatever the reason, probably the easiest way to set up the 1-on-1 situation is by clearing a desired area.

The Area Key Offense affords many opportunities for the clear-out, and any of the players can be isolated at any given time.

For isolating the guards and forward, the best formation we have found is the 1-3-1. It's a standard formation, and many teams may not be aware that you are actually going after a particular man; thus, they aren't likely to "hide" him. Also, the regular plays can be run from this formation in case the 1-on-1 moves break down.

When a forward is being isolated on the wing, the base-line man is the key. The side opposite him is the isolation side, so he must be certain to line up properly if a particular man is to be isolated. When we wish to isolate the guard who may normally play the point on the 1-3-1, we just move him to the wing and bring another man out to the point. Diagram 8-5 shows the point man isolated on the right wing. Note O_5 has moved to the left side of the base line.

In this situation O_1 would be given a few seconds to make his move. If nothing worthwhile materializes, O_5 would cross over to Area 3 on that side for the continuation of the offense.

Naturally, any of the players can be utilized on the wing for the isolation. However, we generally prefer not to use our inside men in this position. They do not usually play that far from the basket or at that angle.

Diagram 8-5

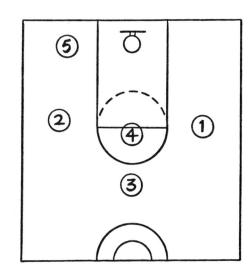

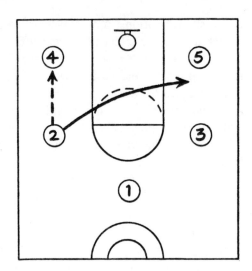

Diagram 8-6

A clear-out from the corner is much more natural, both for them and for the total operation of the offense. In fact, a clear-out occurs spontaneously in the normal operation of the Drop-Step Play.

Diagram 8-6 again shows the pass from Area 2 to Area 3, followed by O_2's cut through the lane. At this point O_4 is left with the whole left side to himself. Whether he decides spontaneously to go for the 1-on-1 maneuver, or it is planned beforehand, the situation is ideal. The move may be made directly from the corner, or it may occur on the way to Area 3. For this reason, the defender may not know whether he has been "set up" or merely "put down."

Don't underestimate the importance of disguising the planned 1-on-1 move. We are obviously going to this situation for a reason. If the opposing coach knows we want it, he is unlikely to give it to us. For instance, there were times when we felt opposing teams were improperly matched with our personnel. In these circumstances, we could gradually "eat away" at them bit by bit, and before they realized what was happening, they were in a poor position to recover. There were other times with the same situation where we were quite obvious about our attempts to exploit particular weaknesses. Adjustments were made which eventually hurt us, because we forced the opposing teams to see their mistakes in matching personnel. You never know what is in another coach's mind when he makes apparently self-defeating moves. Don't worry about it; just leave well enough alone.

In seeking the clear-out situation, therefore, we try not to be too contrived about our formations. There are plenty of chances from the standard formations to yield the desired results.

There are times, however, when the defense makes the first move in trying to hide the weak or vulnerable defender. Since they made the first move, they are obviously "running scared." In this case, we will play psychological "cat and mouse" by trying to force this man into a 1-on-1 situation, even if slightly contrived. Whether he's a good defender in foul trouble or a poor defender who's been found out, he has to be insecure about being told to "hide." He is, therefore, a perfect target to attack. This is the only time, though, that we will depart from our usual patterns and formations to achieve the clear-out.

Picks to the Ball

Our free-lance moves are not confined to the 1-on-1 maneuvers, however. There are many other opportunities and reasons to employ free-lancing in this offense.

Many free-lance offenses have found considerable merit in two-man plays instead of going 1-on-1. These plays rely basically on picks, screens, and rolls.

Most of the two-man plays in this offense involve picks set toward the ball rather than pure screens. (Our distinction between the terms pick and screen have been noted in Chapter 4.) In addition, we seldom use two-man plays involving the man in Area 1. If the offense is properly balanced, any freedom obtained by free-lance picks or screens set by or for this man either leaves the shooter outside the normally desired range or sends the man with the ball into an area already occupied by a defender who can help.

Therefore, the ideal situation for the two-man plays in this offense utilizes picks to the ball, involving the players on the wing and base line.

Diagram 8-7 shows the base-line man (0_4) setting a pick for 0_2, instead of going to Area 3 as expected. If the pick is properly set, 0_2 is free to dribble toward the base line for a jump shot or continue all the way for a lay-up. If 0_4's man switches to 0_2, a roll should be executed by 0_4 (Diagram 8-8).

Another standard two-man play comes after the pass to Area 3. In Diagram 8-9, 0_2 has passed to 0_4 in Area 3. However, instead of executing the cut through the lane, 0_2 goes toward the base line and sets a pick for 0_4. 0_4 can use the move as a screen or continue on for the drive to the

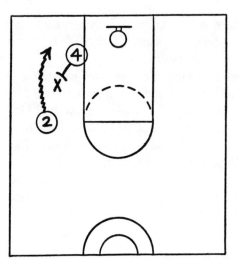

Diagram 8-7

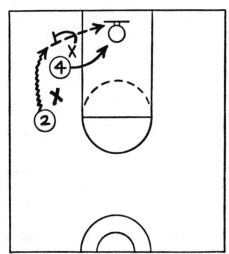

Diagram 8-8

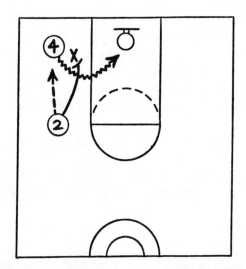

Diagram 8-9

basket. The same situation holds true for the switch in this play. If O_2's man tries to switch to O_4, O_2 rolls to the basket (Diagram 8-10).

The important point about both these moves is that the picks should not be set too far from the basket, as this would place the shooter out of the desired range. This is especially true in regard to the latter of the two plays. The corner man is crowded enough by the boundary lines. Also a pick set too close to the corner will cause O_4 to come up toward Area 2 rather than toward Area 4 or the basket. The angle on the roll is also poor from the extreme corner, as it allows little margin for error on the pass. On both of these plays, the man making the pick should wait until the man with the ball has taken the ball toward him. In the second play, no initial key for a free-lance move is needed as the corner man normally dribbles to Area 4. When he sees the pick waiting, that is his signal. With the first play, it is a little more difficult for the man in Area 2 to know a two-man play is on, and that he should make an initial move toward the basket. Since the base-line man normally moves to Area 3, just the fact that he does not make this move would indicate a free-lance play is being set. If the base-line man hedges up slightly with his arms down, the wing man should sense that he should move toward the basket.

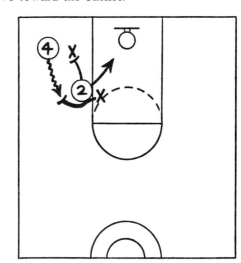

Diagram 8-10

The reason why this particular play is a little more difficult to diagnose at first is that another simple two-man play can be used in a similar situation. As shown in Diagram 8-11, O_4 holds in the low post area rather than moving to Area 3. Instead of heading toward the basket, however, O_2 drops a pass to O_4 in the low post.

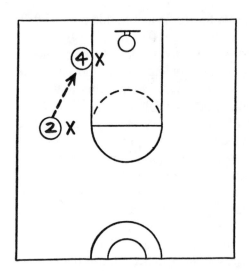

Diagram 8-11

Which of the two plays shall be run from this same situation depends, therefore, on O_4. If he wants the pass in the post, he makes no move toward O_2, and he should hold his hand up high, making it clear that he is ready for the ball. If O_2 misses this signal and starts to drive, O_4 can still move up for the pick, and no harm is done.

Depending upon the personality of the individuals involved, you will probably find the more aggressive of the two initiating the moves. One year the wing man may take the initiative. The next year the veteran base-line man may dominate. This doesn't really hurt your position as this type of situation is not so predictive that any particular members of the defense can rely on it. As the season goes along, and opponents may sense one man being dominant, this may be just when the rookie comes "into his own" and starts taking the initiative. Also, from year to year it gives some variety to your offense.

Still the less aggressive of the two must be ready to recognize instances where the defense may overly concentrate on the stronger of the two.

With the first two plays illustrated above, the switch or double team should lead to a roll by the man setting the pick. With the third play, a different situation prevails.

Normally, the strong threat from the low post will be counter-acted by the double team. O_2's man will usually sag on O_4 once he gets the ball, if he is a definite threat that close to the basket. If this happens, O_2 would merely move down toward the base line in good shooting range, and O_4 would return the pass (Diagram 8-12).

All of these two-man plays work best with formations where there are no other players near that side, such as a high post man. A high post would not directly interfere in some cases, but his defender could complicate the situation by helping out. Then you are really getting involved with three-man plays, and there are several of these which we use, but *we* like to determine when and how they will be run.

Picks Away from the Ball

While the two-man plays usually involve picks to the ball, most of the three-man plays utilize picks away from the ball. The three men involved are the man making the initial pass, the man he sets a pick for, and the man who receives the pass. These plays naturally cover a much wider area of the court and can be run from almost any of the standard formations. These plays also comprise by far the largest number of free-lance options. Though the total number possible may be unmanageable by any one team, the ones most consistent with the general operation of this offense will be presented, and they will be presented in the same sequence as that which the Drop-Step Play takes.

The first of the series concerns possible free-lance moves made after the ball is advanced to Area 2. Normally, the man in Area 1 holds in this

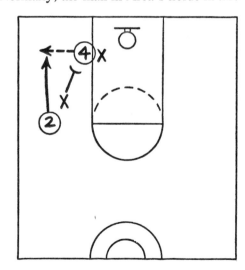

Diagram 8-12

area after the pass to the wing. However, there are times when it is advisable to alter this pattern. As shown earlier, the defender guarding the man in Area 1 may sag or double team the ball coming from Area 3. Though the standard counter-adjusments for this play were already presented, another way to deal with it is to have the offensive man vacate Area 1 after he makes the pass. The defender should follow, or else his man will be running free.

Rather than "waste" this move by simply having the man move from Area 1, he can accomplish other purposes by doing so. We prefer that he set a pick for the man in Area 2 opposite the ball. As shown in Diagram 8-13, O_1 passes to O_2 and sets a pick away from the ball for O_3. Though this is a fairly standard move in many offenses, it is often quite unexpected in this offense, given the usual tendency to hold in Area 1. A simple move, if unexpected, can be quite effective.

You will notice in Diagram 8-13 that no harm is done if the pick fails to free O_3. He just circles out to Area 1 and the positioning remains the same for the basic play.

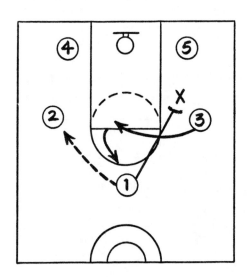

Diagram 8-13

With the ball in Area 2, the man in Area 1 does not always have to make the first move to operate three-man plays. If there is a high post formation, another easy play involves a pick by the high post man for the man in Area 1. Diagram 8-14 shows a 1-3-1 formation where O_4 moves up

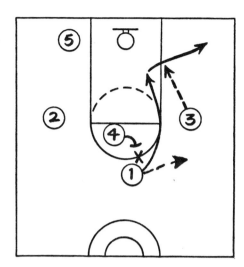

Diagram 8-14

to pick for O_1 after the pass to O_3. If O_1 does not receive the pass, O_4 can step out to Area 1, and O_1 can move on to Area 3 to continue the play.

With these two plays, as with almost all plays involving picks, a roll by the man setting the pick is a standard follow-up maneuver. For this reason, the roll will not be mentioned in the descriptions of the various other plays. It should be taken for granted that the maneuver is workable unless otherwise noted.

The next series of free-lance options is set by the pass from Area 2 to Area 3.

One of the most effective of these options was already described in an earlier chapter. It involves a pick for the base-line man opposite the ball set by the man cutting through the lane from Area 2. This move through the lane is made so often without consequence that when the pick is set, it is seldom expected. As illustrated in Diagram 8-15, O_3 starts toward O_5 as if he is going to set a pick to the ball, then cuts sharply across the lane. This right angle cut signals O_4 to start toward the ball. Again it should be emphasized, that O_3 does not set a pick, but rather makes a normal cut. It is O_4's responsibility to run his man off on O_3. Most officials will not interpret this action as a moving pick.

The players are not the slightest bit apprehensive about using this option, probably because it is almost identical to the standard movements. They may have to be encouraged a little more to use those other options

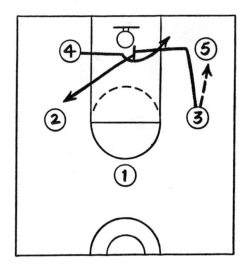

Diagram 8-15

Diagram 8-16

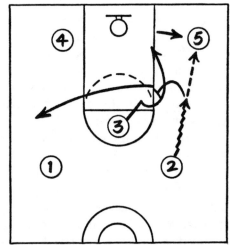

which deviate more noticeably. This reluctance should diminish, the more familiar the players become with the potential of the offense.

It would probably be best to install those options which do not take the player initiating the move too far from the normal path.

For instance, in the 2-1-2 formation shown in Diagram 8-16, O_2 would normally cut through the lane after passing to O_5. Instead, he can modify this cut slightly, without altering it completely, by executing the move illustrated in Diagram 8-16. He starts toward the lane, but circles back slightly to set a pick for O_3. If he doesn't want to wait for a roll, he can just continue on to the position he would normally occupy. Also, if O_3 doesn't receive the pass, he circles out of the area as he does on the standard play.

Once this option is installed, you can go on to some other maneuvers which bear less resemblance to the normal movements. The next two picks away from the ball are useful to break up any sense of tendency or pattern developing in the mind of the defense. However, they can also break up continuity in the offense if the players do not react properly. For this reason, we do not usually like our players to initiate them spontaneously. Though strictly speaking they are free-lance options, we like to utilize them only on instruction from the bench. They may be specifically covered in your pre-game practices and made a part of the game plan, or they may be set up during a time-out. To do otherwise would not mean giving your players freedom so much as inviting chaos.

If the defender guarding the man in Area 1 tends to relax or shift his attention elsewhere when the pass is made to Area 3, we may instruct the man in Area 2 to capitalize on this lapse by setting a pick for the man in Area 1 (Diagram 8-17).

If the pick does not result in freeing O_1 for a pass and shot, O_1 would move through the lane to the weak side. O_3 would step out to Area 1 after the pick. These readjustments would give the necessary positioning to complete the Drop-Step Play.

Diagram 8-17

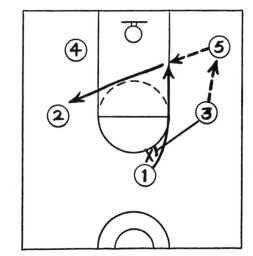

The other three-man play is shown in Diagram 8-18. Once O_3 hits O_5 and begins to make his cut through the lane, O_2 is normally starting to move toward Area 1. Occasionally O_2's man apparently feels he will not be involved actively until the "marriage" forms, as he tends to relax by straightening up and floating casually toward Area 1 in anticipation of the drop-step move. When we notice this, or it is brought to our attention by a player, we will specifically call for this option. As soon as the ball hits O_5, O_1 will wait a count of one and then begin his move toward O_2's man. By the time the pick is set and O_2 makes his cut, the area should be clear, or O_3 would either be through or low enough not to interfere.

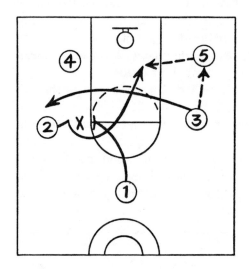

Diagram 8-18

This option makes it difficult to readjust for the normal completion of the Drop-Step Play in the event it fails, since it is hard to achieve the "marriage" without O_5 waiting an undue amount of time for O_3 to circle on out to Area 1. Therefore, we would have to run a single man through for the Drop-Step Play. This is not that unusual in itself, but the weak side would have three men occupying it, as O_2 would have to clear the ball side for O_5. The desired balance isn't there.

Like the preceding play, this one is a designated and often "one shot" maneuver. If the defender gets burnt, he will probably learn a lesson and be more careful. If he is dumb enough to continuously leave himself vulnerable to this pick, we could probably hurt him just as easily on more conventional moves. Nevertheless, an easy lay-up, even occasionally, can upset a team, especially in a close game or in a crucial situation. You may notice a weakness and "sit on it" until the right moment. Then you may spring it and break open a close game. Regardless, whenever you use one of these free-lance options and it yields 2 points, it has done its job. Even if it doesn't lead to a direct score, it may still serve to keep the defense more honest. This, in itself, is an advantage.

Back to the Basic Play

When you consider the wide variety of free-lance options available (the 1-on-1 moves, two-man plays, and three-man plays), even if only a fraction of them yielded a score, this may be enough to win a ball game. As one highly respected coach said, "A basketball game is like a big bag of tricks." Each move you make may contribute only a small fraction to the total game. But when your bag is loaded, and you dump it all out, those fractions add up—hopefully, enough to win.

The other important thing to remember about most (if not all) of the free-lance moves presented here is that they are very low-risk maneuvers. This aspect cannot be stressed too highly. While many offenses which utilize free-lance maneuvers must "sink or swim" with the effectiveness of these moves, this is not the case here. If a particular move fails, no one has to ask "What now?" We just write off the move as a "good try" and continue on with the regular offense. We know what type of shot we want. If we don't get it, there is no need to force a shot for lack of something better to do. There *is* something better to do. Therefore, nothing is really lost by free-lancing within the context of this offense.

One final note should be made of the fact that once there is a breakdown in any of the free-lance moves described above, we revert back to the Drop-Step Play. We do this for several reasons. First, it's the basic play in the offense, and the players should be most familiar with its operation. Also, it is most consistent with the general principles of area progression, and can, therefore, be run from almost any position in which the players find themselves at any given moment. Little or no realigning should be necessary in most instances. Lastly, the other plays are themselves very much like free-lance maneuvers since they operate on the basis of individual decisions to make certain moves.

If, for some reason, a particular free-lance maneuver causes such a drastic departure from the normal movements or positioning that the play cannot proceed in a workable fashion, an outlet pass to any of the outside areas can be made to bring the situation back into focus.

The free-lance maneuvers presented here are by no means an exhaustive description of the total number possible. These are the ones we have found to be most consistent with the general aims of the offense. If you discover others which tend to enhance your own particular situation, it would be foolish to ignore them.

9

Matching Area Key Personnel with Positions

Evaluating Personnel and Your Needs

Whether you are coaching a particular team for the first time, or you are a veteran coach at a school, the first order of business in developing any type of system of play should be a thorough evaluation of the personnel available. Obviously, the veteran coach has an advantage here, as he has seen certain players perform over a period of time and should be fairly well-acquainted with the various abilities of the candidates. However, veteran coaches can often get themselves in an odd type of trap. They may tend to evaluate certain players in terms of past performances and, thereby, operate more on the basis of expectations (or lack of them) rather than actual performance at the time the pre-season practices begin. Granted, a veteran coach who is "close to the situation" and observes his players during the summer (in recreation programs, basketball camps, or summer leagues) and in irregular pick-up games in the early fall, may have a very accurate knowledge of his players' abilities at the opening of the regular practice sessions. He may see some players really develop unexpectedly, while others might show little improvement. All too often though, we coaches tend to pre-judge our talent and rely too much on what we *think* a player's ability ought to be. This prejudice, positive or negative, can color our opinion of a player's actual performance in early season practices.

The new coach is not immune from this prejudice either. In seeking to get an early start, he may review last year's films and/or discuss personnel with others in the school. Again, such evaluations are of past performance only.

For these reasons, it should be a primary goal of every coach to be as objective as possible in evaluating personnel as they perform once the *actual practices* begin and progress.

Though this book deals exclusively with offensive basketball, it would be absurd for me to advocate the choosing of personnel strictly on the basis of offensive ability. The game of basketball must be viewed in a total sense, and most coaches choose their team on the basis of general overall ability.

We feel there are three basic categories within which an athlete's performance should be judged—basic skills and techniques, physical ability, and psychological factors.

In the area of basic skills and techniques, we are, oddly enough, concerned primarily about the willingness and ability of our candidates to play good, tough defense. This is so because we believe our offense can adjust to the players' offensive abilities as they appear. The offense is much more flexible than the defense in most cases, and it is easier for the offense to make the adjustment. Though our offense has been more than adequate, we also pride ourselves in consistently being one of the top defensive teams in the conference. A tough defensive player is usually willing to work hard on offense also. The reverse is not always true.

Other basic skills we evaluate are rebounding, ball handling, shooting, passing, moves with the ball, moves without the ball, and general "court sense."

Though much of rebounding success is due to physical factors, we are interested in a player's ability to "box out" an opponent and keep him at bay. For ball handling, we consider the player's skill in advancing against pressure, changing direction, and using both hands, as well as his speed in advancing the ball. Shooting is evaluated from the standpoint of accuracy, range, quickness of release, and the ability to shoot after movement as well as standing still. With regard to passing, we naturally like our players to master the various types of passes, but we are most interested in determining if a player knows when to deliver the pass, and whether it's received in the proper place at the right time. How it gets there is academic. Moves with the ball are evaluated from the standpoint of competence in freeing oneself for the shot through fakes and drives and ability to utilize picks and screens. Moves without the ball involve this same ability to use picks and screens, as well as individual effort in evading the defender.

General court sense is much more difficult to define and evaluate. Basically, what we are looking for is a player's skill in correctly diagnosing a given situation and acting appropriately in that situation.

All of these skills and techniques are considered as both actual (at the time) and potential. A player may not have a high actual development but may show much greater potential. You should be able to diagnose accurately which players will improve significantly with proper coaching. One index which can help you to determine the amount of improvement possible is an evaluation of physical factors.

Those physical factors which affect performance in basketball and should, therefore, be evaluated, are size, quickness, speed, agility, manual dexterity, elevation (jumping ability), strength, and stamina.

Size is the only one of these factors which is not an ability and cannot be improved upon. But which of us can ignore a player with good size when determining a youngster's potential to help the team? Size may help determine not only a player's success, but also in many cases the position he can play.

However, of greater importance in the minds of many coaches are the physical abilities of an athlete. They may equalize or compensate for disadvantages in size.

As one coach once remarked, "The only thing worse than a big, slow team is a small, slow team." Obviously, he felt quickness and speed were the more important factors. Though quickness and speed may be synonymous to some people, I think most coaches recognize the difference. Quickness deals more with a player's immediate reaction and movement in the short distance, while speed concerns a player's ability to get from one end of the court to another in a given time. Of the two, we personally prefer a quick player rather than a fast one. The amount of times two players get into a foot-race from one basket to the next is minimal compared to the number of times they are involved in a battle to determine who will get the first and vital step to gain an advantage or take it away. Speed is important, though, if you prefer a pressing or fast game or are pitted against such teams.

The agility factor is a bit more confusing, since coaches differ on exactly what constitutes agility. To us, agility is evaluated simply in terms of a player's ability to alter the magnitude or direction of his movements quickly and effectively in reaction to a given situation.

For manual dexterity, we are interested in how well an athlete can control the ball in his possession. Dribbling, shooting, rebounding, passing, and pass catching are all dependent to some degree upon this factor. A player with "bad hands" is operating at a distinct disadvantage.

Elevation can be evaluated from two perspectives—jumping ability on the run and from a set stance. Usually there is a high correlation between the two, but occasionally a player may excel in one category and not in the other. Of the two we feel elevation from a set position is the most important, since most situations requiring jumping involve a set position. Rebounding, jump shooting, and shot blocking all utilize the standing jump.

Though basketball is not supposed to be a contact sport in a pure sense, there is still a large amount of physical confrontation. Setting and fighting picks and screens, making the 3-point play, blocking out on rebounds, "taking a charge," etc., all require physical strength and durability to survive. In addition, strong arms and legs are essential to perform almost all of the basic skills effectively. It's not the most important factor, but all things being equal, the stronger player will operate at a higher degree of effectiveness.

Stamina is closely related to strength as it involves a player's ability to sustain a high level of physical output for extended periods of time. When the final minutes of the crucial game arrive, however, you may well find the initially stronger athlete yielding to the player with greater stamina.

Many of these factors can be significantly improved upon through specially designed programs, but the athlete with a great degree of "natural" physical ability has to figure highly in your initial plans, even if crude in basic skills.

The final element for evaluation—psychological factors—cannot be emphasized too highly. Many potentially great players have proven to be equally huge disappointments because they lacked the proper temperament. In choosing your team and ultimately deciding upon what offense to use, you cannot afford to rely strictly on "talent." You must consider such personal characteristics as drive, determination, aggressiveness, leadership, discipline, self-sacrifice, mental toughness, self-confidence, emotional stability, intelligence, and general coachability, to name only a few.

Does a player enjoy and value competition and want to win (drive)? Will he give up easily, or will he practice long and hard to achieve his goals (determination)? Will he fear physical contact and back away, or will he initiate and relish situations where there may be such confrontations (aggressiveness)? Will he let the situation control him, or will he incite himself and his teammates to control it (leadership)? Is he unruly, or does he abide by regulations regarding his behavior on and off the court (discipline)? Does he put himself above the team, or is he willing to forego his own comfort and ambitions for the good of the team (self-sacrifice)? If he fails to meet expectations will he melt into ineffectiveness, or will he bounce back and be willing to accept criticism (mental toughness)? Will he become upset or indecisive about the unpredictable, or will he assert himself positively (self-confidence)? Will he "blow his cool" at a bad call, a stuffed shot, or a steal, or will he maintain a poised and gentlemanly composure (emotional stability)? Does he require endless amounts of repetition to condition him to a task, or can he grasp his assignment quickly even if complex (intelligence)?

If the rating is affirmative in regard to all or most of these criteria you probably have a highly coachable athlete. He will accept and respect you, the team captain (if he isn't it), team rules, and your system of play. If his rating is negative, he could be the greatest specimen available and yet not help your team nearly as much as a less talented but highly coachable player.

Obviously, very few players will excel in all categories of evaluation, but then few will be totally deficient in all areas. There is a great difference between the ideal and the real. Some players are more specialized in their ability, while others cover a wide range of the desired abilities, but in varying degrees.

There are some combinations of deficiencies we cannot and will not tolerate. But most often we recognize that we will have to put up with the poor ballhandler who may be an outstanding rebounder, or the poor shooter who plays great defense.

Making the Offense Fit the Players

Evaluating the abilities of the athlete is only the beginning. You must then start to add up the pluses and minuses concerning each candidate and determine the strengths and weaknesses your team would have with any given combination of players in the line-up. You can engage in endless amounts of second guessing if you're totally open to any style of play and any combination of players. For sanity's sake, if nothing else, we try to solve the problem of personnel selection by choosing the best all-around athletes, based on the criteria for evaluation listed above. From here we then try to develop a specific attack which will maximize the strengths and minimize the weaknesses of the team as a whole. This situation is especially true in the "rebuilding year," when a large portion of the previous team has gone.

Naturally, the whole situation is made much easier when the nucleus of last year's squad is back. This nucleus may have already developed its own personality and will most likely determine the style of the entire team. If this nucleus is potent in itself, we may then merely try to "fill in the gaps." This is the one time we look for particular players with specific abilities and fit them to the offense. This is not really contradictory to our philosophy of fitting the offense to the players, since the style has really been determined by the proven abilities of the returning players.

Most consistently successful coaches do not play just one year at a time. They generally look ahead and consider the talent of the younger players. Many times a player is groomed for a particular spot, since coaches have a fairly accurate idea in advance of what they will need to complement a team a year from now or more. This eliminates any traumatic adjustments on the part of the player, since he is prepared for the position.

But what if you don't have the powerful nucleus returning, or what if you just can't find someone to replace last year's superstar? Rigid ideas and living in the past are two of the surest ways to eventual obscurity. To have a traditional winner does not require adherence to a traditional style of play. One must be flexible and willing to accept the present crop of players for what they are and what they have to offer.

Another important factor to consider is your bench. Your starting five may be capable of operating under a rigid, pre-ordained style of play, but, if a starter leaves the line-up, will his replacement be capable of sustaining the effectiveness of this style? Will you force him to try to play like someone else or utilize as fully as possible his own special abilities?

As you will see in the remainder of this chapter, the problem of fitting the offense to the players is significantly reduced by the Area Key

Offense. You can operate under a general system which is familiar to your returning players, while minor alterations in formations and use of different options can help you best match the offense with the character and abilities of your total team.

The Area Key Offense will now be discussed from the standpoint of the wide variety of personnel characteristics possible in any given situation.

When asked to fill out a questionnaire on a high school athlete who is a promising college prospect, a question which seems to perplex many coaches is the one which simply asks "Position?" Most of us coaches have been conditioned to the traditional guard, forward, center terminology, but these terms may not accurately describe the position actually played or the duties performed by our players. In our everyday discussions, we may really talk about a pivot man, swing guard, point man, wing man, post man, or base-line man. When asked if a player is a guard, forward, or center, many of us are hard-pressed to actually choose the right term. Since a base-line man may not fulfill the traditional role of a center or guard, we may designate him as a forward. The same is true of a wing man. But what does a guard, forward, or center really do anymore, or where does he play so that we can really distinguish him as such?

The terms originally designated one's position on the court. A guard was in the rear of the attack, a forward closer to the basket, and a center in the middle. Gradually, these positions became associated with certain-sized personnel and certain duties. Guards were generally small, handled the ball well, and shot from the outside. Forwards were intermediate in size, were not required to be excellent dribblers or flashy passers, rebounded fairly well, and shot from closer range. Centers were the tallest men, played near the basket, were tough inside, and seldom touched the ball except to rebound, shoot, or throw the short pass off the "give and go."

Therefore, to eliminate confusion in terminology, we will use these criteria above when referring to the traditional positions, especially the guards, even though it's conceded that they may be misnomers by today's standards.

One-, Two-, and Three-Guard Offenses

A team which has two really fine ballhandlers, who can shoot well outside, is quite fortunate. Usually, though, the only criterion which

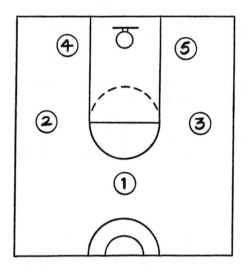

Diagram 9-1

makes most of us capable of saying we have two guards is that we have two small players. When we have only one player who satisfies the traditional criteria for a guard, we should then consider running a single-guard offense.

When the one guard is capable of advancing the ball up court himself and setting up the offense, there are several formations from which you can operate, depending on your remaining personnel.

If you fill out your team with two forwards and two centers, you should seriously consider a 1-2-2 formation, with the low men staying close to the basket as much as possible. Though this formation has been illustrated several times before, I will cover it again here in light of the ideal personnel requirements. You should already be acquainted with the potential of this and subsequent formations.

Using Diagram 9-1, O_1 would be your pure guard. O_2 and O_3 would be the two natural forwards, while O_4 and O_5 would be those players who could ideally play center.

Since you still have two forwards, what you've essentially done is replaced one of the two guards with a second center. Rather than dwell on the disadvantages of having only one guard, you can now capitalize on the prospect of two centers. This gives an entirely different dimension to your offense.

Two-man plays can be executed from either side of the court. This can be done with a single center who floats, but the 1-2-2 gives you additional rebounding strength. It also forces a two-guard opponent into a potential problem in matching up with you defensively.

Another possibility with a single guard is the 1-3-1 formation, one of the most versatile formations in our system. This may be more desirable when you have only one pure center but three forwards. As shown in Diagram 9-2, O_2 and O_3 are the forwards on the wings while O_5 may roam the base line as a "floating forward." O_4 may also alter his position in the post to provide greater variety and movement if he has good moves without the ball and is viewed as a positive threat.

If O_5 is a marginal player—neither a real forward nor a pure center, but a little bit of both—the 1-3-1 can accommodate him very well. He can play the corners and operate occasionally in or near the low post area, but he is not restricted to either.

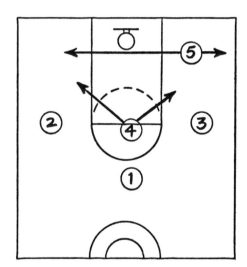

Diagram 9-2

This formation also allows for maximum use of the good driving forward on either or both sides, since a clear-out is easily obtained.

If your center does not have good moves without the ball but is a tough rebounder, the stationary post keeps him fairly close to the basket at all times in a predictable position for rebounding during free-lance moves, rather than having him move about uselessly. While in the post area, he can also serve as a pick or screen for the guard or wing forwards on free-lance options.

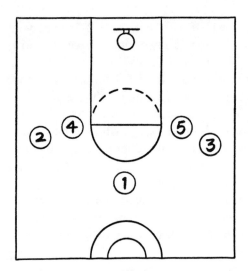

Diagram 9-3

However, some single-guard teams don't have anyone who is really capable of playing the true center position. In this instance, I would suggest trying the 1-4 formation (Diagram 9-3). O_2 and O_3 are the shorter of the four "forwards" and the most maneuverable with and without the ball. They're also the shooters with the best range, outside of the guard (O_1). O_4 and O_5 would be the best rebounders on the team and should remain nearer to the basket.

If you're at a total disadvantage in size, the bringing of your two best rebounders away from the basket, but in scoring range, will force the taller defenders to come out with them. From this position, they will at least have a better opportunity to outmaneuver their defenders for the rebound if the shot is taken before the regular plays are set. If the opponent is both taller *and* quicker, you're in for a long night no matter what you use. But if the taller defenders are slow or awkward, you can gain an advantage by drawing them out away from the basket where maneuverability is more important than size. A 4- or 5-inch height advantage is not nearly so troublesome at 15 feet from the basket as it is at 5 feet.

The 1-4 formation allows the wing men to operate adequately 1-on-1, and also, with the area under the basket cleared of defensive help, the backdoor cuts can be executed almost freely. Then too, the inside men on the 1-4 (O_4 and O_5) serve as natural picks for O_2 and O_3 when the ball is passed to the opposite side. Diagram 9-4 shows the pass to O_3 with O_5 then

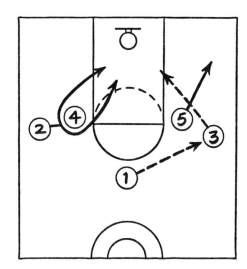

Diagram 9-4

breaking to Area 3. O_2 can go "over the top" of O_4 or fake this move and go "backdoor." Both of these moves are effective free-lance options which do not interfere with the regular offense if unsuccessful.

Though all of these formations are mentioned in terms of the single-guard offense, they should not be thought of simply as single-guard formations. They are equally adaptable if you are forced to put a squad on the floor which really has three guards.

When forced into a three-guard situation, we have always put our best ballhandler of the three at the point, unless he so overshadowed the others in shooting or rebounding that these other talents would be wasted to a great degree. In any event, the player in the point position would have to be capable of advancing the ball effectively and maintaining the poise and discipline necessary to begin our offense.

If the three guards are complemented by two big men, it would probably be wisest to use the 1-2-2 formation with two guards on the wings, since the rebounding strength is where you want it. Also, either guards or forwards can execute from the wings with almost the same effectiveness in the operation of the basic plays. In addition, some of the free-lance options by the inside men may operate more effectively, since the wing guards should be expected to pass inside a bit better than some forwards. Any height advantages should be somewhat neutralized, with the wings playing far from the basket.

The real exchange should amount to an increase in quickness and maneuverability versus a decrease in rebounding power. With the 1-2-2 formation, the regular operation of the offense should keep at least one, and usually both, big men near the basket.

If the three-guard set leaves you with only one big man and one forward, it would probably be wiser to move your remaining forward to a base-line position and go to a 1-3-1. This keeps the one big man near the basket, while the forward is free to roam corner to corner.

Since a guard is expected to be quick, the 1-on-1 moves from the wing can be liberally used in free-lance play by means of the clear-out.

In fact, most of the advantages of the 1-3-1 with a single guard offense can be applied to a three-guard situation.

The same is true of the 1-4, only you are replacing the two outside forwards with guards. With no pure center in the line-up, your two best rebounders should be closest to the basket, only far enough away to draw the bigger defenders out from their most effective position. The main difference between a one-guard and three-guard line-up with no center is that the height disadvantage is probably total. However, the same equalizers that apply to O_4 and O_5 with a one-guard set described above, apply to all four men in the three-guard offense. The probably taller defenders on O_2 and O_3 are also forced to operate farther from the basket where height is not as great an advantage as maneuverability.

In essence, then, what you can really say for the 1-2-2, 1-3-1, and 1-4 formations is that they are operative not so much from either a one-or three-guard offense but an *odd* guard offense, whichever it may be.

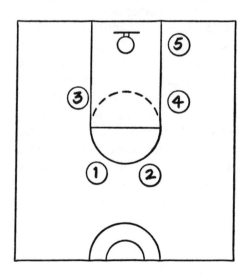

Diagram 9-5

The even guard formations are something entirely different. They apply here only to the normal *two-guard* offense. Though one- and three-guard offenses are really quite common, it is almost miraculous to find a team which would be forced to play four guards and still operate effectively. Even if it were offensively feasible (which is hard to imagine), it would probably be disastrous from a defensive standpoint. Besides an obvious (and probably insurmountable) disadvantage in rebounding, there would likely be at least one and probably two disastrous mismatches on defense.

There are numerous ways in which two-guard offenses can be employed, depending, of course, upon the nature of the remaining players.

One very rare situation in high school, but not uncommon in college today, is the team with three big men capable of playing inside. A team which does use three players of this type will almost out of necessity use two guards since they could expect most teams to press them constantly. They would, therefore, need two excellent ballhandlers.

Though many coaches using three players of this type might move one or two of them to a forward position, there are ways to use all three inside without any real forwards in the line-up.

One such formation is a tight 2-2-1 shown in Diagram 9-5. The two high posts play even with the foul line and just to the outside of the lane. The low post always lines up on the side of the ball.

To run the regular play, either O_1 or O_2 could dribble to Area 2, but a "guard over" move shown in Diagram 9-6 is preferable, since it puts constant pressure on the defense to guard against a pass to either high post

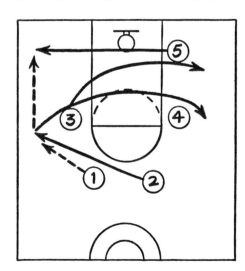

Diagram 9-6

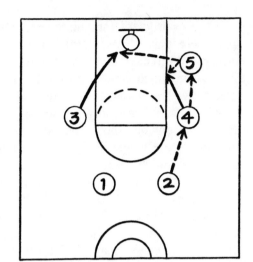

Diagram 9-7

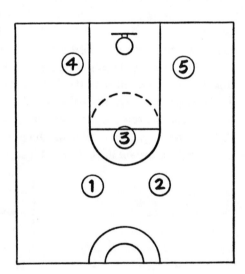

Diagram 9-8

until the pass is thrown to Area 2. The pass to Area 2 can come from a high post as well as a guard.

Since size mismatches should be a problem for the defense, a very simple free-lance option is a direct pass to a high post followed by a "dump pass" to the low post, with both high posts looking for a return pass (Diagram 9-7). The unusualness of this alignment may cause the most initial difficulty, and as a change of pace it can be quite effective.

Another two-guard, triple post formation is the tight 2-1-2 (Diagram 9-8). For our purposes this is more preferable as a basic formation than the previous set, since it is more versatile and leads more easily into the basic plays. The size mismatches and rebounding position are still available also.

This formation has already been dealt with at length in regard to the basic plays and free-lance options, so little more need be said here on these matters. The only additional point of emphasis should be placed on utilization of three legitimate centers versus a center and two forwards, as is normally the case with this formation.

More of the two-man plays can be worked on either side if the guard dribbles to Area 2. Definite attempts should be made to hit O_4 and O_5 in the low post before they move out to Area 3.

The 2-1-2 formation is also ideal for the most traditional offense using two guards, a center, and two forwards. In fact, when the 2-1-2 was dealt with in earlier chapters, I'm sure this is what most of you had in mind.

If O_4 and O_5 (now forwards) are equal in size or taller than their defenders, they may stay tight originally to make best use of their size. If not, they may move out toward the corners to gain more maneuverability.

One free-lance option not mentioned earlier that can be used with two maneuverable, quick-shooting forwards is shown in Diagram 9-9. As O_1 hits O_3, both O_1 and O_2 "split the post" as usual. However, instead of going off to Area 2, they can go low to pick for O_4 and O_5, who would break up off the pick for a pass from O_3 and the quick jumper. If no pass is

Diagram 9-9

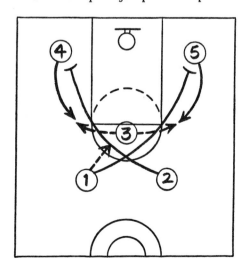

received, O_4 and O_5 can move to Area 2, while O_1 and O_2 would cover Area 3 for the operation of the Drop-Step Play.

If the two forwards in such a line-up are at an obvious disadvantage in size but are definitely more maneuverable than their defenders, a 2-3 alignment would make maximum use of the total team's abilities (Diagram 9-10). The guards are less free to operate toward the wing areas, but they seldom go 1-on-1 from these areas anyway since their dribble is already used by the time they reach the wings. However, the center and forwards have all the room toward the base line in which to operate. Again, taller defenders are drawn out from the basket on the forwards. One-on-one moves by the forwards and center are more viable, while backdoor cuts by the forward are a definite threat.

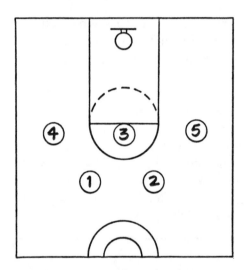

Diagram 9-10

The two remaining situations in two-guard systems are the two-center offense and the offense without a center.

Having two centers is not unusual in itself, but matching the two centers with two guards presents a problem of where to put the remaining player. Most coaches would most likely approach this situation by either making one guard a "swing guard" by moving him to the wing or replacing one of the guards with another forward. However, we are talking about a situation where four of your best players are two true guards and two pure centers.

Since this is an unorthodox situation, it would probably require an unorthodox formation. You should not be totally opposed to such a suggestion if it fits your personnel.

One formation which could capitalize on this situation is a two-guard-out single stack shown in Diagram 9-11. Naturally O_1 and O_2 are the guards. O_4 and O_5 are the big men, while O_3 is the remaining single forward. On the stack side, O_3 can try to free himself for the quick score off O_4's natural pick. If he is not freed for the immediate shot, the Drop-Step Play can be run if O_4 moves to Area 3, or any of the two-man plays can be run to that side. Away from the stack, the play can be run normally, as it would be with the 2-1-2 formation. If one of the big men

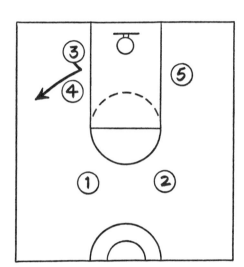

Diagram 9-11

has good moves in the lane, the stack can be reversed (Diagram 9-12), with the big man using the pick by O_3 to free himself in the lane. After the pass to O_4, O_3 would clear the area to allow O_4 room to maneuver. The stack can be set to either or both sides and can be rotated for maximum versatility.

The one remaining two-guard offense is that in which there is no center but three forwards.

Here a 2-2-1 formation may offer the best solution. In Diagram 9-13, O_5 is the tallest and most versatile of the forwards. He is near the basket

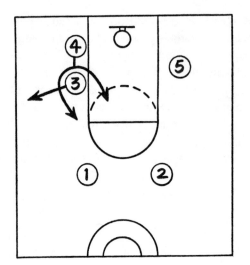

Diagram 9-12

Diagram 9-13

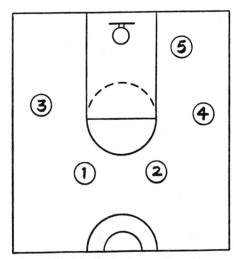

for rebounding and can roam side to side looking for opportunities. He may also move into the post occasionally for variety.

The side opposite the base-line man has the clear-out for 1-on-1 moves and backdoor cuts. The side to the base-line man can work on two-man plays.

By breaking down personnel factors in this manner, I have tried to indicate that certain formations may be better suited to certain types of team characteristics. However, by doing so I did not wish to imply in any way that "multiple formations" simply means that different formations may be used with this offense from year to year, depending upon the type of players you have. Though there may be an "ideal" formation for any given team, we still feel that this formation should only be a basic "bread and butter" set. The maximum responsiveness of this offense is gained from varying formations throughout the course of a game and season, staying away from only those formations which are definitely maladapted to your personnel.

As you will see shortly, substitutions offer an excellent chance and reason to vary formations. But even with the same line-up, variations should be a normal occurrence.

I tried to point out earlier that it's often difficult to specifically categorize a player as being a guard, center, or forward. The more you use multiple formations, the more difficult it becomes. Tell a player he's strictly a forward (whatever your definition is), and make him operate as such, and you'll find him acting more and more like a forward. Don't tell him what he is, and let him operate under different circumstances, and you'll likely find you won't know how to describe him. Even if he isn't that versatile, the offense is, and it can accommodate him. Only when a player has pure and actual ability for a particular position and performs with consistent excellence in that position would we consider it foolish to alternate his positioning. On the other hand, if a player is so inflexible that it appears he can operate only in one position, he is probably not that good at that position anyway. A replacement might not be a bad idea.

Unless you are able to recruit, you are probably unique if you average even one *pure* guard, center, or forward in any given year. Almost all of us coaches can picture the vast majority of our team playing positions different from where they now play, either within a given season or from year to year.

You may also have noticed that all of the formations mentioned thus far have been described in terms of the number of guards. This was done partially because most teams (especially high school and below) seem to have more "guard types" than anything else. But more importantly, this is the one position no team can operate without. You may or may not have candidates capable of playing center or forward, but no team can do without someone capable of playing guard. If the ball can't be advanced or passed accurately inside, the centers and forwards will be rendered ineffective.

Offense with the Big Man

Nonetheless, it's still the contention of most coaches that for a team to really be successful it must have the reliable big man. On balance I would have to agree that, though not totally indispensable, the good, big man is a major necessity in today's game. Not only is the big man a major factor in your rebounding game (at both ends of the court), but a team which can successfully strike inside, at the heart of a defense, is at a tremendous advantage. Outside shooters have their "bad nights," but the good inside man is usually more consistent since he operates at closer range.

Before explaining how to operate this offense with the big man, perhaps I should first explain what I mean by the "big man."

In the first place, the term "big" is itself quite relative. By today's major college standards, "big" might mean anywhere from 6'10" and taller. On other college levels, a coach might consider a big man anyone over 6'7". Some small colleges might find very few players in the conference over 6'6". In high school, 6'6" would be considered a luxury by most coaches.

Then too, I'm sure almost all of us have seen or coached the 6'10" boy who can barely walk and chew gum at the same time. Conversely, we have, probably also seen the 6'3" leaper who dominates such taller opponents inside.

Obviously, the term "big man" is relative. It involves both the situation of your opponents and the individual ability of the player.

Therefore, for our purposes, the big man is defined as any capable player inside who is at least as tall as, or plays as if he is as tall as, the taller players of your normal opponents. In our conference 6'5" is considered "big." In your conference it may be 6'3" or 6'8" and above.

In the four years this offense has been in operation, to date we have had two 6'5" players who would qualify as big men by our definition. Both had been voted MVP in our conference, and both had been selected to the UPI All-State First Team in Pennsylvania. They were great athletes indeed, but we would like to think that the way in which they were utilized in this offense had something to do with their ultimate success and recognition.

The good, big man cannot be underutilized or his abilities will be wasted. On the other hand, if he is overutilized, opponents may mainly concentrate their attention on this player and eventually render not only him but your entire team ineffective. A proper balance must be achieved which capitalizes on his special abilities, but within the context of the total team offense.

When we have the good, big man inside, we put a priority on our offensive attack. We look inside as a primary consideration on free-lance moves.

To give the big man more latitude in operation, we establish three positions in the area of the foul lane—a high post (foul line), a low post (even with the basket), and a mid-post (halfway up the lane).

The inside man also has three speeds at which he may operate in any of these positions. He may stay in a stationary position, which we often use against quicker but smaller defenders. A flashing post may be used when defenders are taller but slower. He may also float or roam with the movement of the ball. This is useful with the lazy defender. It is also helpful against the defender who likes to physically "lean" on the big men.

This movement in and out of various post positions will obviously affect the formation. For instance, a 1-2-2 will become a 1-3-1 if a low post moves high. This is no problem since the offense is geared to changes in formation. The only restriction is that the big man cannot make a free-lance move into an area already occupied. But this is only common sense.

However, we do "bump" our post men occasionally. "Bumping" is a planned maneuver whereby we move one man into an area already occupied while the other man simultaneously moves out. This is done more against zone and combinations than against man-to-man defenses, but it is still employed against the latter. For example, in Diagram 9-14 we change the clear-out side on a 1-3-1 by bumping instead of moving the base-line man across the court. The same formation is maintained, but we may gain an advantage by placing different men in the positions, as defenders may fail to adjust guarding positions.

If the big man definitely operates best out of one side, we usually try to keep him there and place our best outside shooting threat on that side. This prevents sagging inside, or at least it makes the sag very risky. Two-man plays can be worked regularly to this side, taking advantage of the dual threat.

To prevent a one-sided attack from developing, we also like to put a good passer on the opposite side. This makes the flash post to the ball side a positive threat.

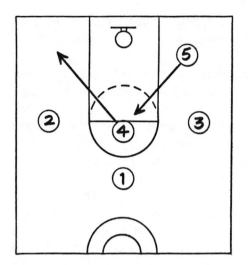

Diagram 9-14

Like most other phases of this offense, our inside game requires a certain degree of versatility on the part of the big man. But it's our conviction based on experience that such versatility can be developed. Execution on any one move may not be perfect, but we feel the difficulty in defending a player from a variety of positions and movements more than compensates for this lack of perfect execution.

Offense Without the Big Man

As you are probably aware by now, the special effectiveness of the big man is derived more from free-lance options and psychological impact rather than anything inherent in the basic plays. They can operate with or without the good inside man. Two of the plays, the Drop Step and Scissors, free the outside men for the shot. The other two, the Bounce Pass Play and the Side Drop Step, give the inside players the shot not as much by virtue of their own special abilities, but through the normal workings of the patterns.

Therefore, if you don't have the inside player who is really effective on his own, one method of attack is to stick more closely to the basic plays and cut down on free-lance options involving the players inside.

For free-lance options, the three-man plays mentioned in the last chapter would probably be your best bet. Most of them are designed for the point guard (if you have one) and wings, while the others can help free the weaker inside men who cannot free themselves. These options are especially good for the player who moves well without the ball.

When you have a player with excellent individual moves with the ball, the isolation options are a natural for him.

If you like to utilize a post man, regardless of his scoring effectiveness, I would recommend the high post formations for you. This will probably draw your opponents' tallest man away from the basket, giving your other players more room to operate from the perimeters on in toward the basket.

If you choose to go without a post man in the absence of the big man, the 1-4 could satisfy your purposes. The 1-2-2 and 2-2-1 are also complementary to this type of strategy if the formations are spread wide instead of keeping the players in tight.

Varying the Offense with Substitutes

You must bear in mind, however, that no matter what type of attack you originally decide upon based on your "starting five," you must be prepared to vary this plan during any given game, depending upon your substitutes.

This point was brought home to us rather clearly one year when our two most reliable substitutes were both 5′8″ guards. Several times during that season we were forced to insert both into the line-up simultaneously. If they had to replace two other guards, there would be little difficulty. However, they often had to replace a big man, a base-line man, or a wing man, all of whom were considerably taller. Fortunately, this offense could accommodate them.

It's ideal to have a capable substitute for each position, but since we haven't had this luxury, we have tried to take a positive approach and capitalize on our situation by altering our formations and adjusting our attack to fit the new circumstances.

Rather than being handicapped by substitutions, we found they offered unique opportunities to vary the offense. If we have been using single guard formations, we might move to two- or three-guard formations. Single post formations might become double post sets, or no post would be used at all.

Too many times we tend to look to our bench only when someone in the starting unit is playing poorly, is in deep foul trouble, or is injured unexpectedly. In reality, though substitutes may not be complete ball players, many of them have special abilities which can and should be utilized periodically for strategic reasons.

With this offense special options can be devised to take advantage of particular abilities, or certain personnel can be inserted, allowing a different formation which can make things happen. With many other offenses, a coach merely tries to minimize the weaknesses brought about by substitutions and hopes the replacements fit into an offense designed around five other players.

After all, almost every player on your bench has some special ability or a combination of less-refined general abilities, or he wouldn't be on the team. Why not utilize these specialties rather than having substitutes try to play like someone else they replaced? A poor outside shooter cannot carry the load for a good shooter simply because he has taken his place in the line-up. However, the poor outside shooter may be a good driver or an excellent passer. By simply changing the emphasis of your attack temporarily, you may avoid the psychological letdown many teams experience when a certain counted-on ability leaves the court with a particular player.

More often than not in crucial games, we have had the refreshing experience of watching a lead held or increased significantly with key personnel on the bench, rather than seeing the lead disintegrate. And this was done with only average overall bench personnel.

Doing Their Own Thing

The key factor here, we feel, is that our substitutes know their strengths and weaknesses, and they don't try to play like anyone else. They do their own thing, and we think we have the offense which allows them to do it.

In fact, this "do your own thing" attitude pervades the entire team. Not only do we accept the highly individualized style and ability of each player, but also we generally encourage it if it's not disruptive of team goals or exhibitionist in nature. We like to allow each player the freedom to do what he does best.

In all honesty, I must confess that most of the free-lance options and individual moves described thus far in this book occurred originally as a result of the personal initiative of our players, rather than any specific direction on the part of our staff. Our major function was that of blending these moves into the total offense.

One of our outstanding inside men, impatient with the normal opera-

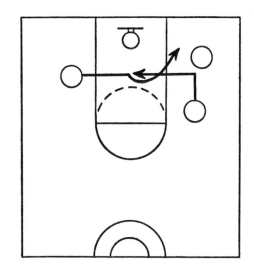

Diagram 9-15

tion of the offense in its primary stages, perfected the flash post move, which added a new weakside dimension to the attack. We subsequently developed the Side-Drop-Step Play to give more continuity to this move.

Another player decided to hold in the post after a stack rather than move to Area 3 when the pass hit Area 2. This gave rise to the Scissors Play.

The right-angle cut shown in Diagram 9-15, which keys the pick for the weakside post man, came about in practice one day when two of our starters suddenly huddled and decided to "screw up" the second defensive unit.

No doubt by the time this book reaches the market, we'll be using options not even thought of as yet. As a result, this book will never be completed in total concept since the Area Key Offense is a never ending thing. As long as new players arrive with new abilities and ideas, this offense will continue to grow. However, the players must feel free to experiment and improvise. We feel this offense offers not only the opportunity to do so but the security which encourages even the apprehensive player to do his own thing.

This chapter dealt with matching the personnel to the offense. I have tried to be specific enough to give some idea of the possibilities which are available to a wide range of circumstances. Conversely, I have tried to be general enough to show how each of them, with its own possibilities in personnel, can be dealt with in an individual manner.

I would expect and hope that each of you will find unique ways of utilizing your own personnel to their maximum efficiency. Any suggestions offered are just that—suggestions. They are not hard-and-fast rules.

Remember, though, just as you ultimately wish to be your "own man," your players deserve the same personal consideration for self-expression in many cases. Put your personnel in a mental and/or physical straight-jacket, and you may eventually find yourself operating in one, with this or any other offense.

10 | *Controlling Game Tempo*

Importance of Controlling and Varying Game Tempo

In some sporting events such as the 100-yard dash, there is little reason to be concerned about regulating the rate of activity or motion at which the athlete operates. He is always expected to operate at full capacity.

However, in contests which involve an extended period of time and where strategy plays at least as important a part, if not a greater part, than pure physical output, one should not only be aware of the importance of tempo but should actively seek to control it.

Basketball is such a game. It is the type of contest that is far too long for the athletes to operate at "full steam," and the outcome of the game is usually highly dependent upon strategic maneuvering rather than just the pure physical prowess of the contestants.

This is not to imply that physical ability is not important, or that a team can be poorly conditioned and still operate effectively. What I do wish to make clear is that some inabilities can be compensated for, while certain abilities of opponents can be partially, if not totally, neutralized. Also, even a superbly conditioned team cannot count on simply overpowering its opponents with brute speed and force. There are elements to this game which transcend these physical factors. One of the most important of these is tempo, and every effort should be made to control it.

By controlling tempo I mean that *you* consciously set the pace or rate of activity at which the game is played, be it fast, slow, or somewhere in between. Sometimes a game inadvertently evolves into a pace at which your team operates at maximum effectiveness for that situation. But why leave it to chance? Why not draw up a game plan which includes tempo as a factor you deliberately seek to establish on your own terms?

Just as you weigh the importance of certain offensive plays or whether a zone or man-for-man defense will be more effective, you should also consider the effect a fast or slow pace will have on your opponent and your own team.

In scouting our opponents, we always try to determine the tempo at which they operate most effectively or the tempo they seem to want to establish. The two are usually synonymous, but occasionally our opponents' game rivals will set a pace at which they appear uncomfortable, but still manage to operate in. Even in those circumstances, the opponent we are scouting will still exhibit tendencies toward one tempo or another.

Their game opponents may be stalling, and they may play along, but we can still tell if the opponents we are scouting want to "open up," since they'll try to do so whenever they get the chance.

Unless a team has developed a predictable style over a number of years, you'll probably need more than one scouting report to determine any true tendency toward tempo.

Once this tendency is determined, we then decide if we're capable of meeting them on those terms. If both of us seem to enjoy the same tempo, we decide who is likely to be better at this type of game. If we feel they are, we will try to alter their tempo. If the reverse is the case, we'll play them on these terms. If the basic styles are opposite, we generally try to play our game, unless we feel we're definitely superior. Then we may play along simply to gain experience at another tempo, if, and when, we're forced to employ it. In all situations, however, we determine what tempo we will accept and what we will not, and do our best to establish the desired tempo during the game.

Many teams seem to try to actively control tempo only late in the game. Then they may desperately try to speed it up (if behind), or slow it down (if ahead). However, to relegate the importance of controlling tempo simply to those late game situations is to grossly underestimate its ultimate importance throughout the entire game. If you worry about tempo only in the final minutes, it may be too late to bother.

There are differing theories on how to control game tempo. Many coaches feel that tempo is set and controlled by the defense. According to this theory, a pressure or sagging defense can speed up or slow down an opponent as desired. There is much to be said about the importance of defense in influencing tempo, but in my view it's just that—influence. It's the offense which ultimately can control tempo. When you have the ball, you're the boss. A press may try to influence you to speed it up, but you can still "walk it up" if you so desire. If a team likes to set up a sagging defense, you can always try to beat the defense back to your basket. Of course, it's probably best to assert that a proper combination of offense and defense is most effective in controlling tempo. But of the two, the offense should be the most important factor, if executed properly.

Most of the remainder of this chapter will, therefore, be devoted to a description of the different rates of offensive attack and how the Area Key Offense can be used to control each of these rates of attack.

Before getting down to the specific speeds of operation, however, some mention should be made of the importance of varying game tempo.

If you're highly conscious of tempo throughout a contest, you'll obviously have some overall rate in mind which you'd ideally wish to establish. However, situations occur during any given game and from game to game, which may cause you to alter this basic plan. You should still try to maintain control of the tempo in light of these changing circumstances, though it may mean a deviation from your basic plan. Nevertheless, if you're flexible in your approach to tempo, you'll be in a much better position to establish ultimate control.

One of the most obvious reasons for varying tempo is the necessity to pace your attack simply to conserve the energy of your players. If you've operated at full speed for much of the contest, and your players finally seem somewhat fatigued, you normally have two choices. You can call frequent time-outs, or you can substitute freely to rest the first unit. However, if neither of these alternatives seems satisfactory for one reason or another, a third alternative is available. You may slow down the tempo temporarily and allow your players a chance to regain some of their strength. If you vary the pace periodically from the beginning of the contest, your players may never find themselves pressing the limit of their endurance. They should always be able to give that "final burst" when needed.

Another reason for being ready to vary tempo concerns attempts of your opponent to set a different pace than you desire. Don't forget, when they have the ball they can control the tempo, if they have a mind to. You might have to play along until the game situation changes to the point where you can control the tempo on your terms.

For instance, if a team is slowing the game down, you may have to wait until you gain the lead in order to force them from the stall, if you can't do it defensively. The same is true if you desire to slow down. You can hardly afford such a tactic if you are behind by more than a few points.

The flexible team will usually be able to establish the desired tempo if it only has the patience to wait for the proper moment.

Next you must consider strategic weaknesses which periodically occur unexpectedly, both for yourself and the opponent.

Suppose you felt you couldn't fast break an opponent and, therefore, planned a more deliberate attack. At some point in the game, the opposing coach tries to "beef up" his rebounding and inserts taller but slower players or crashes everyone to the boards. Would you be willing and able to capitalize on this change by speeding up your attack?

Conversely, what if the player who has triggered your successful fast break gets into deep foul trouble? Will you continue to run without the competent replacement to make the running game effective, or will you slow down temporarily and protect your lead until the key player can be reinserted? I have seen some swift-moving teams go into a virtual freeze to protect a lead until it was safe to bring a certain player back into the game. There are times when you may have little choice but to alter your tempo temporarily.

About now I can imagine many of you thinking of the effect an alteration in tempo can have on existing momentum. Certainly, when you have a team "on the ropes," it may be disastrous to change the tempo, since this can kill your momentum. But, as I say, you may have no choice at times.

Then too, you must realize that the relationship between tempo and momentum should be a two-sided one. If a change in tempo can slow your own momentum or even kill it, then the same should apply for an opponent. If the momentum is going against you, why not try a change in tempo as a means of killing theirs and starting your own?

It's rare to find two highly diverse rates of attack existing simultaneously throughout a contest. One usually yields to the other's style eventually. If things are not going your way anyway, why not try an alteration in tempo? Perhaps the other team will change to your style. You have little to lose by trying.

The last reason to be dealt with where a variation in tempo is desirable is the late game situation where you must seriously consider the clock. This is the time when even the most inflexible teams, tempo-wise, are ready to consider a change. Regardless of the rate you've employed up to this time, a 5-point lead with a minute or two remaining definitely calls for a freeze, unless a panic press is yielding lay-ups. Conversely, a similar deficit at this time requires a no-holds-barred approach.

Again I must repeat, however, that to wait until these last five minutes to seek to gain control of tempo may be too late, especially if you are not used to varying your rate of attack. It's wise to test your ability to freeze the ball and keep the opponent from doing so earlier, if only by going for the "last shot" late in a quarter or half and challenging an opponent who tries to do the same.

Even if you don't find these arguments for in-game variations convincing, you should at least consider varying the tempo game to game. To set out to play every team at the same tempo implies a belief that every team is exactly the same and can be attacked accordingly. This is ridiculous. The only other explanation is that a coach is so confident in the superior ability of his team that he feels he can force everyone to play his style. This is so unusual as to be almost equally ridiculous.

But even if it were the case, there are still reasons to consider a variation in tempo.

First of all, there is always the real possibility of injury to key players. If these players are essential to maintaining the desired tempo, some alternate game plan must be drawn up, unless you want to try to operate on abilities that aren't there.

Whether through a loss of key players to injury or normal circumstances, there are always the various possibilities of the physical mismatch to consider. Against some teams you may be smaller but quicker, while at other times you may have size but not quickness. These differences should require a varied approach in regard to tempo, among other things.

The other reasons for varying tempo from game to game are more strategic than situational.

To vary tempo regularly throughout the season eliminates the development of noticeable tendencies. Teams which operate mostly at one tempo are easier to prepare for. In fact, they may find opponents attacking them on that basis alone—a desire to change or upset this tempo. To operate at one tempo indicates that a team either can't or won't play at any other rate. Such a team is ripe for attempts to alter this tempo.

The psychological impact of having to suddenly reverse one's style of play is too much for some teams to overcome. Some fast break teams "fall apart" if made to slow down, while some deliberate teams find themselves totally incapable of keeping up in a fast-paced game. Psychological inflexibility can be even more detrimental than physical limitations in many cases.

If you anticipate at least the remotest possibility of having to alter tempo occasionally, it's probably wise to gain practice at varying rates of attack. In those "easy" games when you have established total control of the outcome early in the contest, you have a perfect opportunity to practice those rates of attack you may not normally employ. If, and when, you do need to operate at these rates at some future time, you should have not only gained a psychological willingness to do so, but also the game condition experience necessary to operate somewhat efficiently.

I can recall playing on a team where we were really forced to press and desperately fast break an opponent only once the entire year, very late in the season. We had practiced this type of game occasionally throughout the season, however, even though it wasn't a regular part of our style. When we did finally employ it in a moment of dire need, we turned a 7-point deficit into a 4-point victory in less than a minute-and-a-half. I hate to think of the outcome if we had never employed that rate of attack just for practice at earlier times.

Unfortunately for many teams, their offenses are geared to operate primarily at one rate of speed. To vary tempo often requires a change of offenses as well. It's understandable, therefore, why many coaches are reluctant to readily alter their rate of attack.

With the Area Key Offense, you will have no such difficulty in varying tempo. In fact, I cannot think of any other offense commonly known which offers more opportunity to control the tempo, whatever you desire it to be at any given time.

Though we may be consciously concerned with tempo at all times, the ultimate goal of this and every offense is to put points on the scoreboard. The factors which control the tempo, then, are the types of scoring opportunities we look for, and the frequency with which the various maneuvers described earlier are employed.

The Normal Pace Attack

In our "normal pace" attack, a shot is usually taken anywhere from five to 15 seconds after the ball crosses mid-court. The time difference results from whether the plays are run to completion or a free-lance maneuver yields a quicker shot.

This reference to the amount of time it takes to get off a shot is not meant to imply that there is some definite period of time in which a shot should be taken. When operating at a normal pace, this just happens to be the usual range of time it takes to get free for the good shot.

Almost every move in our arsenal is open to exploitation in this attack. However, the free-lance moves are all run within the context of basic plays (after they are set in motion).

We originally set out to run any and all of the regular plays, but once the plays are set in motion we are ready to capitalize on all of the free-lance options whenever they arise.

Since there's no specific time limit placed on the operation of this type of attack, you may feel that it doesn't really aid in controlling tempo. However, to think of tempo only in terms of specific time sequence is to underestimate its importance. The point is, there are times when you are not particularly interested in excessively speeding up or slowing down your rate of attack, but merely operating at a pace where your offense is most versatile. If this pace happens to be flexible, and after examining the situation you find that it's acceptable, then you are still operating at the pace you desire. The concept of tempo need not always imply a somewhat constant rate over a given period of time. You may choose to establish a constantly variable rate as your means of controlling tempo.

Nonetheless, there are times when a more specific and predictable rate of attack is either desirable or necessary.

If the tempo must definitely be picked up and maintained at that level, there are two possibilities—the fast break and the quick-strike attack.

The object of both of these attacks is to get off the best available shot in the shortest time possible. The fast break attack operates on a full-court basis, while the quick-strike offense is used primarily in those situations where we feel it is best to first set ourselves at half-court before going for the shot.

The Fast Break

Though some teams fast break from out-of-bounds after a made shot, as well as after the defensive rebound, we confine our regulated fast break to rebounding situations.

The exact manner in which we run our fast break isn't that important here, as it doesn't have much effect on the matters of ultimate concern in this chapter.

However, there is one point about our fast break that does have some relevance here. We don't assign specific lanes to specific players as some systems do. This requires very predictable defensive locations, and it's usually done to make the transition from last break to normal offense more effective if the break fails. With this offense it really doesn't matter so much whether certain players are in definite positions if the break fails, since the regular offense can continue to operate smoothly, regardless of player positioning.

In resorting to the fast break, the hope is that a good shot will be gained from the break itself. If the break ends unsuccessfully, the outlet pass is thrown to the nearest open area. Though the normal offense picks up at this point, we try to go for the quickest option maneuver available, if forced by game conditions to score swiftly. If not, we may simply write off the fast break as a good try on that possession and settle down to the normal pace until the next possession, when we will go for the fast break again. In fact, in this latter situation, we may even reset our offense and move to a specifc formation rather than utilizing the one we find ourselves in at the time the fast break ends.

In the first situation, though we may be trying to control game tempo by speeding it up, the real determiners of our decisions are the game conditions themselves. We don't like to operate the fast break when we feel compelled to do so. We much prefer to operate it voluntarily. This way our half-court options are more open. If the fast break fails to control the tempo as desired, at least we're in control of conditions under which our offense otherwise functions.

Quick Strikes from a Set Offense

The fast break is not the only way to speed up tempo, however, as was mentioned earlier. The second alternative is the quick-strike attack.

While the fast break is used after acquiring the defensive rebound, the quick strike is used on other changes of possession—violations or offensive fouls by the opponent, jump ball turnovers, made fouls and goals.

After such changes in possession the ball is advanced up court as quickly as possible (to Area 1, ideally), and the earliest possible scoring opportunities are sought.

With the normal pace attack you will recall that all free-lance options occur *within* the context of the basic plays, meaning that the plays are first set in motion before the options are tried. With the quick-strike attack, the situation is reversed. Scoring options are sought before the basic offense begins its operation.

For this phase of the offense, the most useful formation is the double stack, leading to the 1-4. Though it might normally take longer to set than some other formations, once you set your attack to this pace the players should be conscious about setting up quickly. Therefore, the formation is often set much more quickly than might be expected.

From this formation two specific options are best suited for the purpose of this attack. The first is the quick shot for the low man coming off the stack (Diagram 10-1).

If both O_2 and O_3 rub their defenders off clean on the high men on the stack, they should be free for the jump shot immediately. This is the first option to explore.

As soon as either O_2 or O_3 receives the pass, there's no reason for the high man in the stack to the ball side to remain in this position. He does not serve as a screen but only as a pick.

Diagram 10-2 illustrates the desired movements to the ball side. As

Diagram 10-1

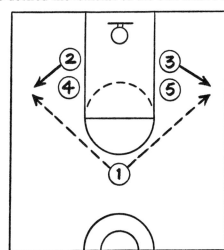

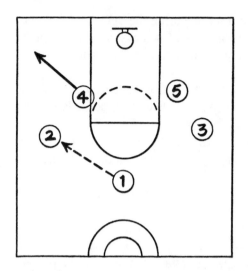

Diagram 10-2

O_2 receives the pass, O_4 proceeds to Area 3. If the quick jump shot is not available, this move by O_4 sets the stage for the second option.

If O_2 doesn't take the shot almost immediately upon receiving the ball, O_3 then uses O_5 (who holds in his position) as a pick to free himself. The most common move executed here is a quick cut "over the top" of O_5's pick, which was already described in an earlier chapter. (See Diagram 5-7.) This move often frees the cutter for an easy lay-up. If the defense executes a switch to pick up O_3, then a roll by O_5 often frees him inside.

Another variation useful against teams which try to get to the top of O_5's pick is for O_3 to start toward the top and then go backdoor (Diagram 10-3). If a switch is executed in this instance, a roll may not work, but there could very well be a mismatch with O_3's man on O_5.

Whatever the outcome of any of these options, the basic plays can always be run afterward.

Another quick-strike formation is the 1-3-1 with the 1-on-1 moves to the clear-out side offering the best opportunity. However, this formation will not yield the desired results in this case, unless you have the really reliable 1-on-1 player. Otherwise, you may simply be wasting valuable time.

Though most of the quick strikes come from options outside the basic format, the one standard play which often hits as quickly as any option, if not more so, is the Bounce Pass Play.

This play works best from the 1-2-2 formation, which is not a standard set for the quick-strike attack. Nonetheless, this may be a good one-shot try, called during a time-out or a break in the action.

Like the fast break, the quick-strike attack may result from necessity more than choice. In this case, you may not be able to risk the 1-2-2

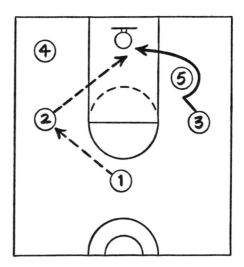

Diagram 10-3

formation, since it doesn't always lend itself to quick scores, except for the Bounce Pass Play which can't be run time and time again.

But then this situation only points out more clearly why it's necessary to gain adequate control of tempo originally so game conditions won't force you to utilize patterns which limit your potential effectiveness.

Of course, playing a speed-up game out of necessity rather than by choice almost always involves a situation whereby you are behind and are forced to catch up quickly. By the very nature of these circumstances your options are limited, and you must face this fact while making the best of it.

Deliberate Basketball

Playing a deliberate style of game is an entirely different situation. Though it's no easier to effect a deliberate style of attack than a fast-paced attack from a technical or executional standpoint, it is much easier in regard to the use of available options. With no pressure to score immediately, even the slowest-evolving and least productive options can be tried with full knowledge that, if they fail, nothing is really lost, so long as you maintain possession.

Obviously, only the normal attack offers the full range of options at all times, since the fast speed attack denies the slower-evolving options, and the deliberate attack, by nature, will seek to avoid the hastily conceived options. Nevertheless, the deliberate attack is still capable of using all the available options, at least in theory, if and when the situation is right.

With the deliberate style of attack as we define it, we are not interested in eating up time. That is the purpose of the stall and freeze. To be deliberate, as we conceive it, is simply to consider most carefully the maneuvers we exploit. While we normally look for the good shot, in the deliberate attack we take only the *best* shot. Where the 15-foot might ordinarily be acceptable, only the 10-foot shot or closer might now be considered. Where we might normally let a player try to thread the needle on a pass, we will now ask him to hit only those players who are definitely open.

In this attack we look primarily to the basic plays for our shots, since we feel they yield the best shot most predictably. Though certain options may give us better shots on occasion, they might also yield closer but harder shots to make. Whether the potential shot comes after an option maneuver or the completion of a standard play, the player with the ball must decide if he is definitely confident he can score. If there's any doubt, the ball is given up to another player, and we continue our attack until the proper shot is available.

In essence, the deliberate offense is a very low-risk form of attack. Therefore, it usually takes longer than usual for the best shot possible to materialize, even though no time limit is placed on taking the shot. Though individual possessions may yield the quick score, over a long period of time you'll find that the deliberate attack is useful in slowing down the game tempo.

The extent of the "slowdown" really depends upon the ability of the defense. If, even in the deliberate offense, you find your team has little difficulty in scoring quickly, you probably don't have much to worry about in terms of the outcome of the game.

However, you must be aware of those highly efficient offensive teams that employ a "sieve defense" temporarily in order to get you in the habit of swift movement. Suddenly the "sieve" closes, and you don't have the great open shot, but you're moving too fast offensively to consider the difference in defense.

One major college coach told me of his experience with such a high-powered offensive team. He intended to slow them down with a deliberate offense but found the good shot came so easily that he let his team score whenever they could. Over 100 points were scored in the first half of a game that was supposed to be played deliberately (on his team's behalf). But his team was still ahead at halftime, so he let the tempo continue at this pace. Suddenly, late in the game, the opponent cut off the really good shot, but he could not make his team adjust to this change. They still fired up the quick shot, only farther out. When the smoke finally cleared, his team lost a game in which a total of over 200 points were scored.

The Stall and Freeze

Though the deliberate attack normally slows the game down, possibilities to the contrary must be considered. If you wish to avoid this other possibility by not only going for the "pure shot" but also placing a time factor on the shot, it would probably be better to consider a tactic we describe as the stall.

In our scheme a stall is defined as that type of attack whereby a prescribed amount of time is used before a shot is even considered, regardless of available possibilities (except for an unmolested lay-up). After this time period has elapsed, whatever has been designated, we move into our deliberate attack.

If 20 seconds appears to make the opponents "itchy" and throws off their timing, then that's the period of time we will allow to elapse before moving in. If it takes longer then we'll take longer.

There are also other situations where the stall is effective in controlling tempo.

As mentioned earlier, a key offensive threat may leave the line-up temporarily due to foul trouble. Occasionally a minor injury or even an illness which limits his stamina may also force him to leave the game for a time. You may try to continue on with the same style of attack without him, if you have a highly capable replacement. If not you may be able to "kill" additional time on each possession with the stall until he can re-enter the game. At least this might help you maintain the status quo. The opponents often hope that when the key threat leaves the game they can crush the offense and take control. When the stall prevents this, there may be a psychological letdown for the opponents which also aids your cause.

The other place where the stall might prove useful is that point in the game where you wish to definitely "sit on a lead," but you feel it is too early for a complete freeze. If you have a 10-point lead and can kill 30 seconds per possession, you may have the game locked up with four minutes to go, even if you fail to score the remainder of the game. If you still can average close to a point per possession from the stall, you may begin to sew it up as early as the five-minute mark with that 10-point lead.

Few of us would have the guts or ability to "let the air out" completely with five minutes to go, and, by the time the one- or two-minute

mark comes, that 10-point lead too often dissolves. The stall can eliminate much of the discomfort associated with making the decision as to
when to start "actually sitting on the lead." You can start with a stall and
gradually ease into the freeze when you definitely·feel more comfortable
about using it.

The form the stall takes in this offense depends upon the type of
defense being employed. If the defense is content to sag, even late in the
game, we'll work the perimeters as much as possible, especially Areas 1
and 2. While doing so, we may flash people in and out of the post to give
the impression we're trying to go inside. By doing so, the defense may
not get suspicious if we don't follow with our basic movements. They
may think we've shifted entirely to an inside effort. Occasionally the
flashing post may be hit, but instead of going directly to the basket, the
post man would merely throw an outlet pass to the perimeters. After the
designated time is up, we can then go for the "sure shot" by whatever
means it occurs.

A 1-3-1 is also consistent with this type of play, as you can act as
though you're looking for the good 1-on-1 move, which never seems to
come. The sides are then reversed until we're ready to move in for a
score.

Against teams that are employing pressure defense on the half-court,
either because it's their normal style of play or they sense your strategy,
the form of the stall changes significantly. We generally line up in a
double stack to free the pass to the wing and go through the entire pattern
of the Drop-Step Play, except that the shot is not taken until the desired
time has elapsed. Once this time has passed, and the deliberate attack
begins, the best shot will be taken whenever or wherever it occurs.

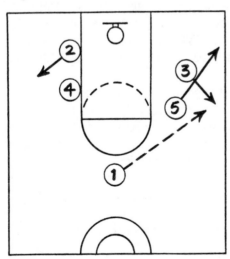

Diagram 10-4

Since it normally takes about 10 seconds for the Drop-Step Play to be completed and reset again, you can use this time period to gauge your strategy. If you want to kill 30 seconds, you would run through the play three times. You can also signal verbally or with a designated sign when you wish the stall to end.

To achieve better continuity on the stall from the double stack, we usually alter the pattern of the play slightly. These alterations are shown in Diagrams 10-4 through 10-7.

When O_1 hits O_3 in Area 2, O_5 moves to Area 3 as usual. However, O_4 remains stationary in the post on the weak side throughout the play. After the pass to Area 3, O_3 cuts through the lane as usual. But instead of continuing on to Area 2 on the weak side to replace O_2, who goes to form the marriage, O_3 settles behind O_4 as the low man on the stack. Then, after O_5 moves to Area 4, the drop step is always made by the outside man (in this case O_2). Instead of O_1 going to set a pick for the weakside post, he goes behind O_5 as the low man on the stack to that side. When O_2 receives the ball, he dribbles back to Area 1 and starts the same play on the other side.

The defense can seldom prevent this pattern from continuing, for in order to overplay on the drop-step move at the foul line or above, they'd be risking a possible lay-up if the offensive man broke to the basket. This move is almost invariably conceded. Since, I think, it was already shown how the other movements in this play can operate effectively against pressure, there should be little reason why the entire sequence cannot operate as expected.

The stall, operated as described, has an advantage which goes beyond mere control of tempo. If it's executed properly, the defense may

Diagram 10-5

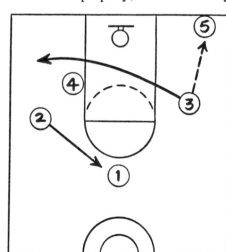

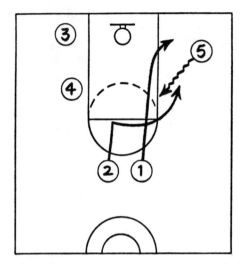

Diagram 10-6

Diagram 10-7

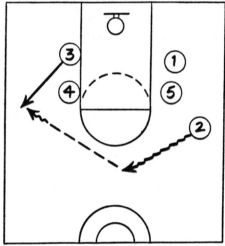

think you're really trying to freeze the ball. In this case, they might concentrate strictly on stopping the movement of the ball, thinking you're not looking for the shot. They may, therefore, be totally unprepared when you actually do begin to attack from the same pattern. Just as they appear to be on to your movements, you suddenly go to the basket.

If they choose to stop ball movement only, they could easily be conceding the shot when it comes. If they choose to guard against the possible shot, they usually have to concede ball movement outside. In either case, they're in a very difficult position, since they don't really know how long the stall is designed to last. By varying the time of the stall, you can further increase the uncertainty.

If the stall is properly executed, the true freeze may never be necessary, since the given lead may be maintained or increased. Nonetheless, there are times when you want no shots taken under any circumstances, except the uncontested lay-up. When that time arrives in a game, where you feel confident that you can maintain possession until the end, the ball is worth whatever lead you have.

There are several methods for freezing the ball which have proven successful—weaves, continuity passing patterns, various four-corner spreads, etc. Though we don't doubt the potential effectiveness of these freeze offenses, we do question the advisability of using them.

Anytime you depart from your normal offensive patterns to incorporate a specialized offense into your system, you must realize that a partial duplication of time and effort is involved here. It takes time to teach and learn this special offense, and it must be worked on periodically to insure its proper execution. Little of this is really beneficial for the overall operation of your offense. It's not a case of time "wasted," so much as time that might be better spent on something else.

You can't save time only working on the special offense with your first team either. Quite often the team on the court near the end of the game is different in part than the one which started. Since the freeze requires the utmost in execution to be really effective, you should practice it with several different personnel combinations likely to occur late in the game. With a different specialized offense for the freeze, you might find yourself spending much more practice time perfecting it than you can afford.

Another reason for not deviating from the basic patterns for the freeze involves diagnosis by the defense. Once you go into a different pattern, your intentions become immediately known. Since every second literally counts when freezing the ball, the longer it takes for the defense to know what you're doing the more time you kill.

Once the diagnosis is made, the defense may go "all out" to stop the freeze. In putting extreme pressure on the ball, the defense may leave openings elsewhere. With familiar patterns in operation, your players should spot such openings much more readily. With somewhat different patterns, they may not.

One final element to consider is pure and simple panic. Though the freeze should put pressure on the defense, once the defense begins to pressure wildly it is occasionally the offense which ultimately panics and falls apart. When normal patterns are used, the defense is less likely to pressure wildly than rely on their standard means of stopping the patterns. Even if the defense does pursue at a frantic pace, the offense should feel more secure and settled in knowing they're basically running the normal offense.

Aside from the almost complete reluctance to shoot, the only thing that distinguishes the freeze from the stall is a slight alteration in the spacing of the drop-step move.

As shown in Diagram 10-8, the drop-step cut is made well above the foul line instead of having the marriage go even with or below the ball to set up this cut. Whenever a freeze is in operation, there's always a danger of a double team involved in bringing another offensive man too close to the ball. The early execution of the drop-step move prevents this double team from forming effectively.

Though the basic pattern can be rotated from side to side, it can be kept to one side only if you choose to do so. If you're forced to have a weak ballhandler in the line-up, you may want to keep the ball away from his side as much as possible. Though it's unlikely that you'd have to keep a poor ballhandler in the game, it is a definite possibility that one or two of your players are poor foul shooters. If the opponent's tactic is to send you to the foul line, hoping for the miss and rebound, you don't want these players in possession of the ball. If your best foul shooters can't always have the ball, at least you're worst foul shooters don't have to touch it any more than is absolutely necessary.

The entire time this freeze is being carried out, the basic offense can still put constant pressure on the defense. Any foolish gamble, lapse in thought, or relaxation underneath could easily result in a lay-up.

Using the same patterns to control all the various types of tempo leaves the defense somewhat uncertain as to what your exact plans may be. A normal attack can be slowed to a stall or freeze almost without

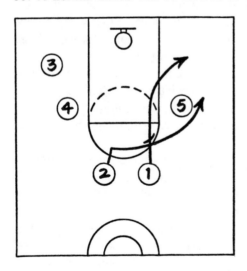

Diagram 10-8

noticing, while an apparent stall or freeze can be opened up to a full-blown attack at will.

This potential can make any given type of attack that much more effective.

As one coach remarked, ''In basketball you play your opponent part of the game and the clock the remainder.'' It's so much easier to have one offense which allows you to do both.

11 | *The Area Key Offense and Other Half-Court Defenses*

Lest the title of this chapter becomes deceiving, one point should be made clear. The Area Key Offense was conceived for use against man-for-man defense. It was never really intended to be a kind of universal offense, designed to attack any and all types of defenses.

Though I sincerely wish I could someday come upon an offense which proved to be equally effective, regardless of what defense an opponent could throw against us, I really doubt this possibility is realistic. There are simply too many different types of defenses, all operating on different principles, all exhibiting definite strengths and weaknesses.

Certain offenses may be *operational* against all types of defense, but that is not the same as saying they are equally effective against every defense. These offenses obviously work better against some defenses than others.

Since the offensive ideal is to get the *most* out of an attack at *all* times, the "universal offense" would fall short of this ideal.

Though I argued against the use of "specialized offenses" in the previous chapter, I would hardly consider a particular offense for zone defenses a specialized offense. Half your game time may be spent attacking zones. This would certainly not fall under the category of special situations, as a freeze would be.

For these reasons, if we are definitely pitted against a zone defense, we will generally switch from the Area Key Offense to our standard zone attack, described in Chapter 12.

Nevertheless, there are times when certain of the basic *concepts* of the Area Key Offense are quite useful in attacking half-court defenses other than pure man-for-man defenses. Therefore, it's the purpose of this chapter to explain how your experience with the Area Key Offense can aid in overcoming certain problems with other half-court defenses.

Though the overall offense is not employed, specific elements are chosen when applicable.

Countering the Half-Court Trap

The first defensive ploy which can cause considerable difficulty is the threat of a half-court trap press. The half-court trap press can be devastating at times. Ironically, though, it's usually less troublesome if applied constantly. In this instance, you can develop an attack to counter the traps, and employ it steadily throughout the contest. The real difficulty comes when this defense is employed only periodically and unexpectedly.

You obviously have a particular formation which you use to attack this defense. If this formation is different from the one you normally use against a straight man-for-man or zone defense, the problem is clear. If you anticipate the trap and form up against it, you'll have to reset if the trap never appears. This is difficult for some teams. If you choose to ignore the occasional threat of the half-court trap and line up in your usual formation, you may be caught off-guard periodically.

Naturally the former approach would be safer, but your players may either think it overcautious or unconsciously fail to line up in what is usually an unnatural formation.

If your players are used to operating with multiple formations under the Area Key Offense, these problems of attacking the trap at half-court are not nearly so menacing.

When we anticipate the half-court trap, we merely inform our players that we'll always cross the mid-court line in our standard formation for that purpose, which happens to be 2-1-2. Since we use this formation regularly, our players assume it without hesitation—no questions asked.

If the trap never materializes, we can simply operate our offense from this formation (the concept of multiple formations applies to our zone offense as well as man-for-man).

If they don't press, and we feel another formation would be more successful against the standard defense they're employing, we can just as easily reset our formation, since we're used to such changes.

Diagram 11-1 shows the formation we use to attack the half-court trap press. The trap press presented is a standard 1-3-1.

Assuming O_1 has the ball as he crosses mid-court, X_1 and X_2 will try to apply the trap. If X_4 comes up to stop the return pass to O_2, we'll try to hit O_3, who can wheel around and look for O_4 or O_5 going to the basket (Diagram 11-2). If O_3 is not open, we go to a familiar move. O_1 hits O_4 and O_3 wheels out of the post toward the basket (Diagram 11-3). This maneuver is used after the pass to Area 3 in the regular man-for-man pattern. Not only is the formation similar to the one used in the Area Key Offense, but also there is a carry-over in subsequent movement as well.

If X_4 does not try to shut off O_2, we will pass to him and look for the same options to the other side.

Once the press is broken, we will move our 2-1-2 in closer and operate with it in a normal pattern. If the defense falls back to a man-for-man, we're very much on "home ground." If they fall back to a zone, we have other patterns for that as well.

Though most teams resort to a zone after trying for the trap at half-court, it is not uncommon to find a team go to a man-for-man late in the game when the trap fails. They may feel the trap is their best chance for getting the turnover, but being behind, they cannot afford to settle into a zone. To keep up some degree of pressure, the man-for-man is employed.

If the defense shows a tendency toward this, each man will have to match up with the offensive man nearest his area. Otherwise, a player can run loose until the proper match is made.

What we do here is chart the pattern of the match-up. We will then try to position our men in such a way as to gain an immediate mismatch.

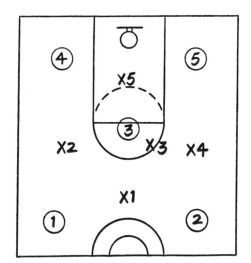

Diagram 11-1

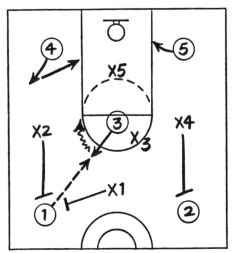

Diagram 11-2

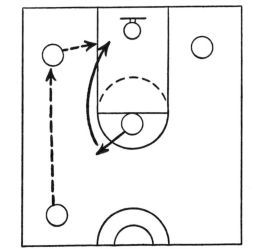

Diagram 11-3

Simply having two men switch sides may be enough to gain the desired mismatch. If alternating assignments is necessary, this is not beyond our ability, since assignments are often rotated in the Area Key Offense.

This is the general plan of attack when the trap does occur at half-court. But what if it fails to materialize and you'd rather not operate out of the formation designed for the trap? The transition to another formation must be smooth, especially if a man-to-man defense is waiting. If your players are accustomed to making such transitions, this task is much easier.

Naturally, though, as with any in-action switch in formations, the form this transition takes will depend upon your personnel and which players you eventually want in certain positions.

You should first begin by evaluating the needs of the first formation, then designing the direction of the realignment according to the demands of the second formation.

For example, if you want to go from a 2-1-2 half-court press alignment into an eventual 1-2-2, you should first position the players as to their ability in attacking the press.

As positioned in Diagram 11-1, O_1 and O_2 are the two best ballhandlers; O_3 is the most agile and versatile big man; O_4 and O_5 are the best outside shooters and drivers (excepting the guards), whether they are normally forwards, base-line men, or a combination of the two.

Assuming O_1 is the better ballhandler of the two guards, we would want him to take the point position on a 1-2-2. O_2 would then become the swing guard. Since O_3 is one of the big men, he would most likely switch to a base-line position. This means that either O_4 or O_5 would have to move to a wing. The shorter and/or more maneuverable of the two would probably take on this assignment. Whichever player this is, it would be foolish to put him on the same side as the swing guard, since that would necessitate one of them moving cross-court to realign. With O_2 as the swing guard and O_4 as the one who will go to the other wing, it's much more sensible to put O_4 opposite O_2.

Diagram 11-4 shows how an ideal realignment would take place from a 2-1-2 to a 1-2-2 under these circumstances.

O_1 goes to the top of the key; O_2 swings down to the right wing, while O_4 moves up to the left wing; O_3 goes low on the left side; O_5 remains where he is.

To arrive at a 1-3-1 formation, all movements would be the same, except O_3 would remain in the high post.

Any formation can eventually be arrived at from another alignment. Whether or not the transition is smooth usually depends upon how well

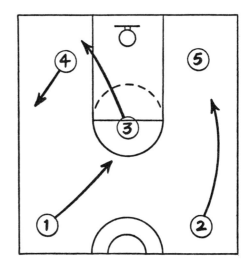

Diagram 11-4

your players are prepared to go from one position to another. It also depends upon your ability to see ahead and take the transition into account before you position them originally.

If you can't go from one particular formation to another without excess movement and criss-crossing, it would probably be best not to even consider such a change.

Attacking Combination Defenses

Another offensive problem is often presented by a group of defenses commonly known as "combination defenses." These combine elements of both man-for-man and zone principles simultaneously. In one type of combination defense, some player or players may be playing strictly man-for-man, while the remainder of the team provides zone coverage. The "triangle-and-2" and the "box-and-1" are the most common types. We consider the "diamond-and-1" a mere variation of the box-and-1. Another type of combination defense is the "match-up." Here you find the entire team alternating between the man-for-man and zone principles throughout the series. A given area (or areas) of coverage is assigned, but within that area the offensive man is played man-for-man. Whatever formation the offense assumes, the defense will take the same basic shape.

These combinations present two special problems for the offense. One is recognition, especially if the opponent is not known for using them. It may take several possessions to determine exactly what type of coverage you're getting. Besides the apparent inconsistency in coverage, some teams are especially adept at disguising their defenses.

The second problem is how to attack a combination defense. Do you play it like a zone or a man-for-man? Or do you devise a special offense just for the various combinations?

We approach the problem of recognition by using the Drop-Step Play. This usually gives you a good idea of the average coverage. Once the defense is diagnosed to be a combination, we reset and attack it accordingly.

As far as the exact manner of attack is concerned, I believe the offense can still take the initiative in most cases. With a triangle-and-2 or box-and-1, you can decide whether or not to "give up" the men being played man-for-man as decoys and concentrate on attacking the remainder of the defense as to the weaknesses inherent in that type of zone coverage. However, unless the opponents are merely trying to upset you with an unorthodox defense, they are usually trying to keep a tight reign on that player (or players) they feel are essential to your success. To constantly decoy these players might be unwise if they really are vital to your success. In this case, you may still want to free them on a man-for-man basis.

Actually, the ideal situation would be one that allows you to do both interchangeably; in essence, to have a "combination offense."

The Area Key Offense can be easily adjusted to this method of attack without having to rely on any special offensive preparation. You need not spend large amounts of time preparing for the combinations, and you need not fear they will force you out of your normal offense.

First the triangle-and-2 will be covered. With this defense, two men play man-for-man, while the remaining three men cover the other offensive players on an area basis. The point of the zone triangle depends upon the men being covered man-for-man. Diagrams 11-5 and 11-6 show two common possibilities.

Without going into any great detail, I will simply say that you probably won't ever see two pure outside men or two pure inside men being played man-for-man simultaneously. This makes the area coverage extremely difficult if a sudden shift in offensive positioning occurs. If two inside men receiving personal coverage suddenly moved outside, and an outside man slipped inside, the remaining men (on the triangle), who were geared for outside coverage, may not readjust for inside area coverage.

Most often you will see a guard-center, forward-center, or occasionally guard-forward coverage man-for-man.

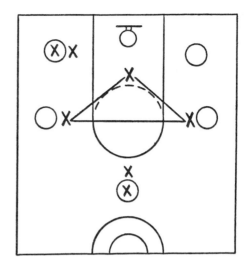

Diagram 11-5

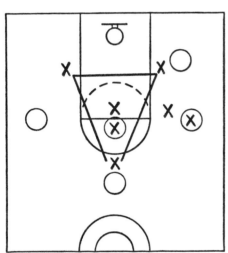

Diagram 11-6

The first way in which the Area Key Offense thwarts the triangle-and-2 is its use of multiple formations. Being never really sure of the offensive alignment, it's difficult for the opponent to divide assignments for the area coverage. If the assignments are predicted on your using a 1-2-2 formation, a 1-3-1 or 2-1-2 could cause considerable confusion.

This won't stop everyone from trying this defense, however. But, if the multiple formations are taken into account, and still they plan to use this defense, you can bet a considerable amount of time must have gone into preparing for the game defensively. This is also an advantage, as less time is left for other phases of the game.

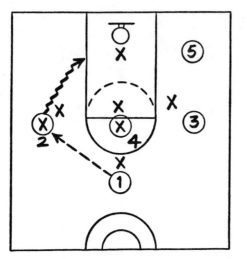

Diagram 11-7

Diagram 11-8

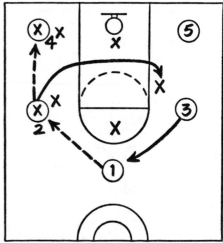

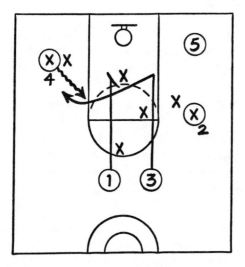

Diagram 11-9

Assuming you do face the triangle-and-2 though, how can it be attacked?

First the attacks predicted on the guard-center and forward-center coverages will be considered.

If you want to utilize the closely guarded men, and you feel they can maneuver 1-on-1, formations designed to exploit this ability should be employed.

Whether a guard or forward is receiving personal coverage, the 1-3-1 can be employed to isolate either of them on the wing. Diagram 11-7 shows O_2 with the entire left side to himself. O_4's man won't provide much help since he's assigned to stay close to his man. The only defender who can cause a problem is the one positioned under the basket. If he steps over to help on the drive, though, O_5 will be free on the other side of the basket. If the man in O_3's area sags to prevent a lay-up by O_5, then O_3 should be open for a good shot.

If you wish to give O_4 a free side, a 1-2-2 should suffice, with O_2 hitting O_4 and clearing out as usual (Diagram 11-8). If there is trouble hitting the wing, a stack can be used to free O_2.

This particular sequence of movements not only clears a side for O_4, but if he's unable to capitalize on this clear-out, the Drop-Step Play can be completed (Diagram 11-9). The same is true for the 1-3-1 isolation.

As long as the wing man to the ball side has man-for-man coverage and clears his man from that side, there is little chance of a double team in Area 4. There's no reason why the play can't be completed.

It's best if the drop-step maneuver is executed by the outside man (O_3) since he's even less likely to receive coverage.

By forcing "zone men" to use man-for-man coverage, you're defeating their purpose in using the combination.

Both men being covered man-for-man don't have to occupy the same side on the 1-2-2 either. O_4 could go low to the side away from O_2 as a decoy. The play can still be run because of the clear-out of Area 2 by O_2.

With the guard-forward coverage the 1-3-1 isolation should apply again, with either of the two taking the clear-out side. The Drop-Step Play should also work here as a follow-up.

However, the Bounce Pass Play is almost "tailor made" for this situation. As shown in Diagram 11-10, O_1 and O_2 have drawn man-for-man coverage. With a pass to O_3, if O_1 and O_2 go to set a double pick for O_4, their men will follow. This will clear the middle for O_4. A switch is very unlikely, since there is only partial man-for-man coverage.

Of the three combination defenses listed, the triangle-and-2 is the least common. However, each year more and more teams appear to put

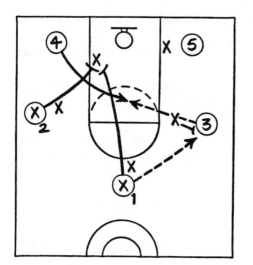

Diagram 11-10

Diagram 11-11

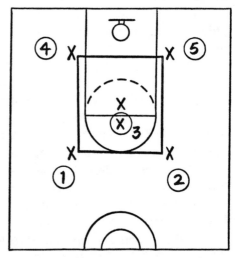

this defense in their repertoire. You may not see much of it, especially if you show a balanced offensive attack. Nonetheless, it's wise to form a mental picture in advance of the types of options you have available through the Area Key Offense.

A more commonly used combination defense is the box-and-1 or diamond-and-1. Here only one man plays straight man-for-man, while the other four play zone. Whether the positioning of the other four is in a box or diamond shape really depends upon the offensive alignment. In Diagram 11-11, a two-guard offense necessitates a two-guard front defensively. If a single guard is used, and he splits the two front men on the

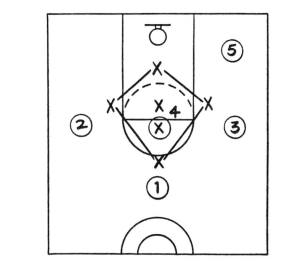

Diagram 11-12

box, one of them must declare. The other one should then drop off to cover a wing. The effect, therefore, is that of a diamond (Diagram 11-12).

Though a thoroughly prepared team will usually be ready to play as either a box or diamond, some hastily conceived attempts at this defense approach it only one way.

For this reason, once this defense is diagnosed, we see if they want to play it as either a box or diamond. We then try to force them into the other form. If they fail to adjust, there will be easy openings. If they make the change, they may not execute the slides properly. With enough offensive movement there is usually a lapse somewhere, and the good shot is available.

For the purposes of this chapter, though, we'll assume that you're attacking a well-prepared team who can play either a box or diamond interchangeably.

Since the man-for-man coverage can be applied to any player with this defense, the options for guard, forward, and center will be explained.

Though the defense is different than the triangle-and-2, the offensive approach can be much the same. However, the effect of a given approach is not always as predictable. With a triangle-and-2, the movements of two defenders are certain—they will follow their men. With the box-and-1, you can only be sure of one man. Therefore, you have to anticipate the adjustments of four others instead of three. Nonetheless, you can still narrow down the defensive options to a level where an adequate attack can be planned.

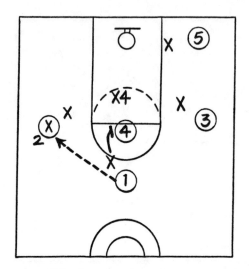

Diagram 11-13

Whether guards or forwards are involved in the single coverage, the wing isolation can still be attempted. Still, it can't be as easily guaranteed. As Diagram 11-13 shows, an attempt is made to isolate O_2 on the wing. If X_4 does not follow O_4 up to a high post, he can prevent O_2 from driving that side. However, the defense must be gambling that O_4 can't hurt them. You can always look inside, taking the opening they give. If O_4 is an adequate inside threat, you will either have the isolation you desire, or you can chew them up inside.

If the isolation yields no results, and the inside isn't open either, the next move is to send O_5 across the base line. Here's where the defense may commit a vital error. Whether they're playing the zone from the original standpoint of a box or a diamond, X_5's area probably doesn't extend to the opposite side of the foul lane. This is especially likely in the diamond coverage. If X_5 releases early on O_5, he may be open just as he comes out of the lane. O_2 should look for this pass first. When O_5 does not receive this quick pass, he goes to Area 3, and the Drop-Step Play is set in motion (Diagram 11-14). Once O_2 clears the side after the pass to O_5, the way is clear for movement to Area 4.

If a guard is covered closely, and you wish to employ a two-guard front, the 2-1-2 (Diagram 11-15) is adequate in setting up the Area Key moves. This formation is useful in getting the ball to your guard when the opponents are denying it on the wing, since they're not likely to deny that far out. It won't give you a clear-out situation, but there's still a good amount of room to operate in.

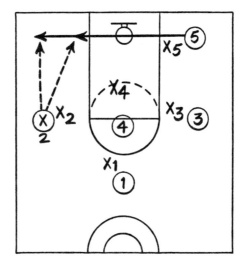

Diagram 11-14

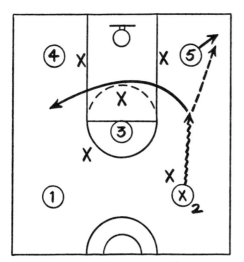

Diagram 11-15

The Drop-Step Play can also be set easily by having the guard dribble to Area 2, pass to Area 3, and clear the side.

Another possibility is a direct pass to the high post and a double cut off the post (Diagram 11-16). O_2's man will follow closely, but still may be picked off on the play. X_1 may have the most difficult time. The cut by O_1 may exceed his area of normal coverage. It's quite likely that he won't follow O_1 to the other side of the lane. If the split doesn't free anyone, O_3 might at least be able to get the ball to O_2 again on the wing (Diagram 11-17), and the Drop-Step Play can be run from there.

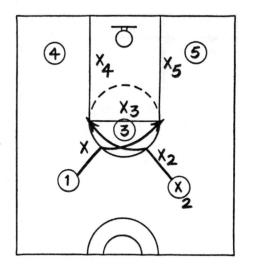

Diagram 11-16

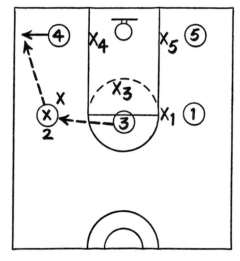

Diagram 11-17

There's one point about completing this play with a high post in the formation that should be covered. The high post naturally rolls out of the area, as in the man-for-man play. There is no guarantee the defender in his area will follow though. If the defender does go with him, the area is clear, but when he doesn't, there's a good possibility the post man will be free underneath. In Diagram 11-18, X_3 holds in his area. The only other man to pick up O_3 underneath is X_5. He may prevent O_3 from scoring, but it's unlikely he can prevent the pass to O_5. With X_5 going for O_3, there is no one available to cover O_5 on the other side. He should be open for an easy lay-up.

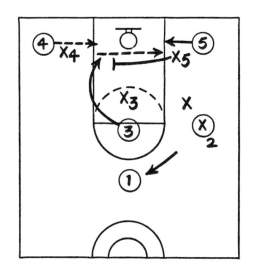

Diagram 11-18

These may seem like a lot of plays to cover for a special defense, but really they are only the standard plays and free-lance options you should be using in the man-for-man offense. It's the defense which should be concerned with the variety in movements.

This point can be illustrated further. With a forward receiving personal coverage, much the same format can be followed with the 1-2-2 or 1-3-1 formations. Occasionally, though, you can add another standard formation—the 1-4, and the options from it—without any special preparations.

The formation in itself is bound to cause immediate difficulty in the zone coverage. This difficulty can be exploited on a free-lance basis early in the contest.

Assuming adjustments will be made, however, there's one frequently used man-for-man option from this formation that has to present special problems for the defense without any offensive preparation necessary.

In Diagram 11-19, O_1 hits O_3 on the wing and O_5 moves out to Area 3. X_5 must follow, at least part way, so O_5 won't be totally free on the base line. Once this move is made, O_2 goes over the top or behind O_4's pick. A total switch is not likely since X_2 has probably been told to stay with his man wherever he goes. It's more likely that X_4 will hedge out and try to help, or you may even get double coverage on O_2. In either case, O_4 should be alert for the possibility of a roll.

The final sequence of movements against a box-and-1 involves man-for-man coverage on the center.

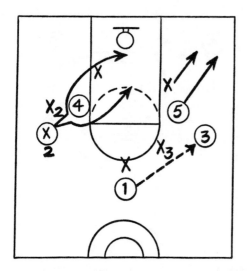

Diagram 11-19

Because the perimeters receive zone coverage, it's quite difficult to run the basic man-for-man plays. However, the box-and-1 is most difficult to execute on the post man, for if he's good enough to require a special defense he's probably hard enough to stop. Unlike men playing the perimeters, who must usually make some forward movement with the ball after they receive it before they can shoot, the inside man is extremely dangerous by just receiving the ball. He's already in the heart of the defense and close enough for the good shot. Besides, he's probably used to operating with close coverage normally.

In fact, to operate against a box-and-1 on the center is not much different than facing a normal zone, since everyone can play much the same way. The center just has to work harder. But the close coverage on him personally leaves less maneuverability for the rest of the defense. In my opinion, the defense should have the more difficult time in adjusting.

For this reason we rely mostly on our zone attack against this variation of the defense, except for a few simple options.

One is a low post pick shown in Diagram 11-20. When the pass hits O_2, O_4, who is receiving the man-for-man coverage, goes across the lane to pick for O_5. Again it's unlikely that a switch will occur since X_4's assignment is to guard O_4 wherever he goes. O_5 is often so wide open that his biggest problem is staying calm enough to make the unmolested lay-up. This may sound facetious, but we've had players so shocked they got overanxious and blew the shot.

If O_5 is not immediately open, he continues on toward the corner. X_5 doesn't usually follow him past the lane. If he does, we'll reverse the ball, pull O_4 out of that side, and send a man into the vacant area.

Another free-lance alternative is to run two-man plays with O_4 in the low post.

These moves, in conjunction with the regular zone attack, are usually enough to get most teams out of the box-and-1. We have never faced a team that stayed with this defense or the triangle-and-2 for more than one period at a time.

If you don't feel comfortable against these combinations, but still have a slim lead, one final alternative is available. Hold the ball out front and force the opponent into a straight man-for-man defense. This rarely fails. These combinations are hardly good for pressuring an opponent into giving up the ball.

Though the box-and-1 and triangle-and-2 can be troublesome temporarily, they should eventually break down during the course of a game. There are many technical flaws in both defenses and few teams employ them regularly. Even if they did, the form the defenses take against your team would be different than against another team. Therefore, you can usually count on the fact that limited preparation went into either of these defenses for your game. This should intensify the technical flaws already present.

By using many of the same components from your basic offense, you should be on home ground. If you're the type of team which may be subject to either of these defenses, you should anticipate in advance which players would be tailed man-for-man and adjust your plans accordingly. For all these reasons you might not burn them so badly in the beginning that they get out of the combination quickly, but you should be

Diagram 11-20

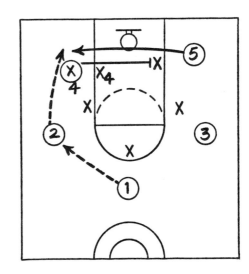

able to eat away at them to the point where they must abandon it or face certain defeat. Seldom should one of these combinations cause an inferior team to defeat you. And these are the teams which use them the most!

The final combination defense to be covered, the match-up, is an entirely different matter.

Though it's often complex to operate, there are *very* few technical flaws. If it breaks down consistently, it's usually due to a lack of execution, not inadequacies in design. Also, once the principles are learned, this defense can apply to almost any team. Consequently, any team which takes the time to install a match-up usually does so with the intent of using it regularly, not once or twice a year. You can bet it's practiced constantly and usually executed quite well.

Even with the advance knowledge of scouting reports (which you don't have on the other two combinations), we still feel a good match-up is the toughest of all the combination defenses to crack systematically. We've virtually given up on trying to find system-wide technical flaws. Instead, we try to concentrate on individual failures in execution. This takes extreme patience if the entire team is sound and failures are only temporary. Here we just try to cause enough defensive movement until someone is a little late getting into position. On the other hand, if we feel we've found one consistent individual weakness, we'll work it to death until they stop us.

In any event, we prefer to attack the match-up as if it were a zone, rather than a man-for-man. Because basic area assignments are part of the match-up, it's difficult to count on a complete clear-out for 1-on-1 moves, though a 1-3-1 may yield enough room to operate with some forms of this defense. But you can't dictate the situation; you can only take it when it's there. For the same reason, it's hard to clear the areas where the basic plays are completed.

Nonetheless, there's considerable carry-over on several of the basic elements of the Area Key Offense, as many of them are applicable against the match-up.

First of all, the match-up is designed to do just what the name implies—match up against whatever formation appears. Still, most match-ups originate from the standpoint of a particular defensive alignment (1-2-2, 2-3, 1-3-1 are the most common). This is necessary as a frame of reference from which the matches are designed. Rules are given for moving from this alignment to the formation the offense assumes.

The more formations you employ, the more rules there are to be applied. If there's even a slight delay in matching, someone might be free to capitalize on the confusion. The ability to employ multiple formations is, therefore, a positive asset in this strategy. By resetting after the first match occurs, you may also be able to obtain desirable "mismatches," personnel-wise.

For example, in Diagram 11-21 you originally line up in a 1-2-2. X_3 is their second smallest man and X_5 is their tallest man. Suppose you put one of your tallest men in O_3's position and a smaller, but more maneuverable forward in the low post (O_5). Since it's not a man-for-man, they must match by area as shown. By bringing O_5 to a high post, you should force X_5 to come with him where he may be less effective. After this move is completed, O_3 moves low. In certain match-ups, the smaller X_3 will follow him. You now have a big man (O_3) on one of their smaller men inside where it can hurt them. You also have a maneuverable driver (O_5) on a taller but slower defender. If they try to switch back, you may catch them in the middle of the switch.

There are many such variations you could no doubt devise to fit your own circumstances. Because the match-ups are by area there'll be many mismatches, but most of them away from the basket. It's up to you to ease the defense into mismatches underneath where they can hurt them the most. It can be done if you understand the nature of the match-up you face.

One place where carry-over occurs from the Area Key Offense is in the use of free-lance moves.

Unlike a sagging zone, the match-up is aggressive, especially to the ball side. Men are guarded farther out. Therefore, inside post cuts can often be used effectively. With defenders more on the perimeter, the man

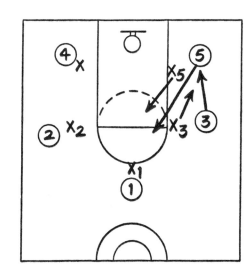

Diagram 11-21

guarding a flashing post is generally on his own. With this in mind, the full range of standard post cuts, described in an earlier chapter, are a basic part of our attack.

In certain formations, two-man plays between a wing and low post are also applicable, especially if the low post man has the edge on his defender.

These ploys by no means exhaust our entire method of attack against the match-up, but having a phase of this attack congruent with the man-for-man offense makes preparation and implementation much easier.

In concluding this segment on the combination defenses, it should be evident that much of our attack is based on the standard moves of the Area Key Offense. For this reason, it takes far less time to prepare for such defenses, and many of the maneuvers can be developed on the spot in most cases. If hit unexpectedly by a combination defense, we're in a better position to adjust than many other teams who rely on more specialized offenses to counter combination defenses.

It's quite possible that you may go through an entire season without ever seeing a combination defense. You must be prepared to attack if confronted with one of the combinations, but to spend large amounts of time and effort on separate preparation may constitute a diversion of valuable time.

Attacking Traditional Zones

However, one half-court defense you can't afford to overlook in your preparation is the zone defense. Unlike the other half-court defenses covered thus far, the zone is a part of almost every team's arsenal. No matter how seriously a team appears to be committed to a man-for-man defense, it would be safe to assume that they could throw up a zone at any time. And you'll certainly see a zone enough during the season that some kind of special preparation is needed to combat it.

As I stated earlier, we have a zone attack separate from the Area Key Offense, and we usually operate entirely with our zone attack (explained in Chapter 12).

However, purely by accident we discovered that a variation of the Drop-Step Play is often quite useful against certain zones. We had seen a man-for-man for most of a particular game, and on one possession set out to run the Drop-Step Play. We hit Area 2 and then Area 3 as usual. The player in Area 2 made his cut through the lane, but the defender followed only to the edge of the foul lane. Before the players diagnosed it as a

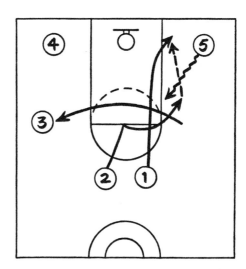

Diagram 11-22

zone, the man in Area 3 started for Area 4 and the marriage was formed. As they started down the lane, the inside man in the marriage saw a defensive player staying at the top of the foul line and gave the signal for the outside man to complete the play. The inside man then went down the lane and back out on the ball side. The outside man received the pass and promptly hit his partner on the base line for an easy jump shot. This play is shown in Diagram 11-22.

The defense was a 3-2, as we later saw on film. We tried this option again on a 1-2-2 zone and found that it worked. It then became apparent that a zone defense with only two men in the back was vulnerable to this play. The outside man to the ball side has to follow the cutter from Area 2 at least to the foul lane. The low man to the ball side has to guard the man moving to Area 4 at least within a few feet of this area. Once the pass is made after the drop-step move, there is no one left to cover the guard swinging down to the base line.

Besides, few zone teams expect to see us running our man-for-man offensive play against them.

Certainly this play won't sustain the offense, but it is useful as a diversion. Perhaps more importantly, the opponent may feel the necessity to alter the basic zone to stop this play. One adjustment is to have the low man drop off the ball coming from Area 3. In this case, the player coming from Area 3 will pause, holding the dribble, until the defender backs off. He then continues on toward the basket.

Another possibility is for the defensive wing man to pick up the dribble from Area 3. In this case, the drop-step maneuver itself will yield the shot.

Whether this play consistently yields a scoring opportunity may not be as important as the fact that you can force the opponent to alter the basic zone slides.

Adjusting to Multiple Defenses

Before concluding this chapter, something should be said in regard to a tactic becoming more and more common every year—the use of multiple defenses. At least once next season you are very likely to face a team which has no main defense, but switches defenses constantly.

One time down the court you may see a zone; the next time a man-for-man. Or several different zones will be used from time to time. In some cases, the switches occur during a given possession. A 2-1-2 suddenly becomes a 3-2 or 1-2-2 by bringing the middle man up to the top of the key.

The theory is that if you have a separate offense for zone and man-for-man defenses, or a different attack for each type of zone, the constant shifts will throw off your offense since you never know what to expect. In essence, it's multiple formations in reverse.

Even though I am an advocate of multiple formations as an offensive strategy, I doubt its effectiveness on defense. Regardless of what formation we're in offensively, the basic movements in the plays are the same. This is not the case on defense as the assignments on each particular defense are considerably different. They are, therefore, faced with learning the principles of five or six entirely different defenses. To use an old cliché; they may very well be a "jack of all trades and a master of none." Besides not executing properly, there may be considerable confusion as to what defense they should be in and what the proper moves are for any given defense.

There is also the problem of keying the switches. One of my former players, now in college, told me it was quite comical one game listening to an opponent constantly ask, "What the hell are we in now?"

One method now used for keying switches is the huddle during fouls or dead balls. Though our opponents frown on the practice, we send one of our men into the other team's huddle. It's perfectly legal! Either this cures the practice of huddling, or we know as much as the defense. Even if codes are used, it doesn't take long to figure them out. The same goes for flags, numbers, or hand signals given from the bench. Keep an eye on the other coach, and you'll soon figure out his plans.

In any event, if a team is switching merely from one zone to another, we set up and diagnose whether it's an odd or even front (one or two men out on the front line). We then shift accordingly. It's much easier for us to change in progress than it is for them.

If the defense runs the entire spectrum, we use a different approach. We start with a zone attack. We generally get enough movement there to determine if they're in a man-for-man. If they're not, we go to the appropriate zone attack. If a man-for-man is apparent, we move into the Area Key Offense full steam.

Sometimes, though, we'll run our Drop-Step Play from the start. As I showed earlier, some options from this play work whether it's a zone or man-for-man.

At other times, we don't even bother to diagnose the defense. We simply match our greatest strength against what we feel is their greatest weakness, and work at it until we gain the upper hand. Many times this has merely been the two-man plays between a wing and low post. Whether they're in a man-for-man, box-and-1, triangle-and-2, match-up, 1-2-2, 3-2, or whatever, they're going to be presented with an almost identical defensive problem.

Of course, the ultimate weapon against any team which insists on switching defenses is to force them to go to one particular defense, namely a man-for-man. This can be done with the standard ploy of holding the ball out front when you get the lead. If they're not in a man-for-man defense they soon will be, unless they go to a zone trap defense. In any event, once you've established your intent, you will have narrowed their options considerably. You'll see one or the other, and you can react accordingly.

Besides, you will have done perhaps even greater psychological damage. Not only will a game plan be destroyed, but the opponents may be forced to play a defense with which they may not feel comfortable.

It sounds extremely superfluous to mention how important it is to get an early lead, even if it's only a point or 2. But some coaches don't seem, to mind much whether they're 2 points ahead or 2 points behind after the first four minutes. They feel their teams will work it out eventually. This may be true, but they don't seem to sense that even a 1-point lead means far more than the mere point difference.

It's not just a matter of points, but an entirely different realm of strategic maneuvering that a lead makes available, especially in dealing with combination defenses of any type and zones. That early 2-point deficit may stay constant if you can't crack the defense. A 2-point lead, on the other hand, may allow you to force an alternation in the defense before it does any great damage.

Instead of playing along and hoping, we would prefer to exercise extreme patience early in the game and go for only the very best scoring opportunity on each possession. If we succeed in gaining the lead, we make strategic moves whenever we feel the time is right.

It's not defeatest to refuse to play against certain half-court defenses. It's only a natural impulse to try to play the type of game at which you feel most comfortable.

We normally see a wide variety of half-court defenses through the year and we've usually been quite successful against them. Outside of being at a pure disadvantage in physical talent, I can honestly say that no particular type of defense has brought us to wit's end. From a technical standpoint, I think we have been able to handle any type of defense we've faced.

As is almost inevitable, however, on some occasions we just aren't as sharp or alert as we should be. In these instances, we would prefer going to the full Area Key Offense if at all possible.

12 | *A Complementary Zone Offense*

$\mathbf{T}$hough the expressed purpose of this book is to present an original and unique approach to man-for-man offensive basketball, it is felt that any work devoted specifically to offense would be somewhat incomplete without at least some presentation of a complementary zone attack.

Not only do many coaches express considerable concern over their zone offense itself, but also they are interested in installing a zone attack which is generally consistent with the basic principles of their man-for-man offense.

For these reasons our basic approach to zone offense is presented here, even though, as was acknowledged earlier, it is admittedly separate from the Area Key Offense for the most part.

It's certainly not antagonistic to the Area Key Offense by any means. In fact, it's quite complementary in many respects. However, it is different and should be approached as such.

Since we have chosen to use separate offenses against both zone and man-for-man defenses, it is probably apparent that we view each type of defense as a separate entity, each presenting its own special problems.

Observations and Recommendations Regarding Zone Offense

Consequently, it would be proper to initially state some observations and recommendations concerning zone offense in general terms.

First of all, it has been our experience that those teams which have the poorest zone offenses are generally those teams which seldom, if ever, play zone defense. There are two possible conclusions to be drawn from this: (1) Many coaches are not familiar enough with zone defense to play it, and therefore cannot communicate its principles and difficulties to the players for offensive purposes; (2) many coaches do not respect zone defense and instill a sense of disrespect for zones in their players, so that when a good zone is presented the offense approaches it with a sense of arrogance that is unjustified and potentially fatal psychologically.

My first recommendation, therefore, is this: If you want to have an effective zone offense, learn and teach, at least to some extent, the best zone defensive principles available with a respectful attitude. By noticing the strengths and weaknesses of your own zone defense, you and your players can see where you can and cannot attack another zone. Nothing is lost since every team should have some form of zone defense in its arsenal.

Secondly, in designing a general attack, don't assume that a defense can't execute a move to cover a given position. You'll have more than egg on your face when you find that a competent zone executes far beyond your expectations. You'll probably have your key maneuvers wiped out as well. When in doubt assume the defense *can* execute.

Thirdly, scout your opponents and concentrate on diagnosing the strengths and weaknesses of the zones they play and the particular ways they play them. There are numerous basic zones, and each team has its own peculiar way of playing each one of them. Openings are present in every defense, however, if you carefully search for them.

Lastly, if you feel your present zone attack is not adequate, don't count on your problems working themselves out eventually. As the word gets around, as it surely does, you'll simply see more and more zones and your difficulties will only multiply.

How to Evaluate a Zone Offense

One of the most difficult problems regarding any type of offense is that of evaluating the effectiveness of a given offense. The most obvious criterion is whether or not the offense puts a large number of points on the board. However, there are two other factors which ultimately affect the number of points you score, and they do not necessitate a negative evaluation of a low-scoring offense. You may be an extremely fine defensive team which forces opponents to control the ball a great amount of time in looking for the good shot. Conversely, your own team may be willing to look only for the good shot and consume time in the process. Two relatively fine offensive teams may, therefore, end up in a rather low scoring contest.

For these reasons we like to evaluate our offensive effectiveness in terms of the number of points we score *per possession*. We feel an effective offense should score *an average* of at least 1 point per possession, and we judge our offense on any given night accordingly. We may score more and lose or score less and win, but in these instances we feel the defense was the deciding factor.

This standard will vary by virtue of the caliber of competition, but it generally serves as an effective yardstick on an average basis over several games or a whole season.

General Zone Offensive Theory

Before any offense can take form on the court, there must first be some theoretical considerations as to what you want your offense to accomplish and how you plan to accomplish it.

The theoretical foundation of our zone attack rests on four simple but basic principles: patience, rapid ball movement, inside penetration and balance.

By patience we mean very simply that we are willing to wait until we get or create the opening we desire before attempting the good percentage shot. Against a well-coordinated and skillfully executed zone defense, this may ultimately break down into a battle of nerves, an attempt to see which side will first lose its patience and gamble. However, in basketball, many people feel there is no such thing as a stalemate. They argue that if both sides reach a "stand-off" the defense wins, since no points are scored. Nonetheless, there are also no ties in basketball. As long as you have the ball, the other team can't score either. In my opinion, in cases of a "stalemate," the offense still has the upper hand. If you doubt this, just consider a tie game in the final seconds with the offense holding out for the last shot. The defense inevitably feels the greater pressure. Its only hope is to close ranks and execute with care and discipline. The offense really only has to worry about the man with the ball breaking ranks, while the defense has five men who must be "kept in line." If any one of the five on defense fails to execute or gets impatient, the whole game could be lost.

Though the point is exaggerated, our players are told that if we control the taps at each quarter, the worst that a patient offense can yield is an overtime game.

However, many teams apparently feel that a patient and deliberate attack means a slow-moving attack. Evidently, their idea of patience is to throw a pass, look over the court, hold the ball for awhile, and wait for the defense to present a flaw. This is not our idea of patience. In no instance is patience equated with speed of attack. It's a quality of a state of mind, not a quantity of physical measurement.

An offense which moves slowly is simply playing into the hands of a good zone defense, for it gives the defense time to recover its position on each pass.

On the contrary, an effective zone offense must move the ball as rapidly as possible in order to force a "lag" in defensive adjustment.

It has been our experience that the ball can be moved faster than any man can move, offensively or defensively. For this reason, we seldom reposition our offensive players by running cutters through or around to any great extent, with the exception of our inside men. Instead, our perimeter players concentrate on rather subtle shifts into the seams of the zone (the area midway between the positon of any two particular defensive players).

Whenever a perimeter offensive man receives a pass, there is one of three basic things he is instructed to do with the ball in short order.

Whenever he is in definite shooting range, his first option is to look for the shot immediately upon receiving the ball. If he is not in range or is closely covered, he then looks to pass to a man closer to the basket (especially in the pivot). If this possibility is closed, he quickly moves the ball to another player on the perimeter. We seldom dribble the ball against a zone since dribbling on the perimeters usually does little more than give the defense recovery time, while driving against a good zone is generally quite difficult. Most competent zone defenses are geared to stop driving penetration as a major consideration.

Nonetheless, inside penetration is essential to destroying a zone defense for it strikes at the very heart of the defense. Even if the inside man doesn't have an uncontested shot, he still has a closer, and therefore, higher percentage shot. However, we would much rather have our inside penetration come in the form of a pass rather than a dribble.

Even if the perimeter man does manage to break through the first line of defense, he still must face "the gut" of the defense before he is "home free." However, he must do so off the dribble since he has already put the ball on the floor to get where he is. If the ball arrives inside on a pass, though, the man with the ball has the full range of offensive moves open to him. He can use all the fakes and drives as well as his moves off the dribble. Besides, the inside man who receives the pass is almost always taller than the perimeter players and is, therefore, better qualified through size and training to effectively combat the inside defenders. He is on home ground in the pivot area. The outside man is in somewhat foreign territory.

In addition, excess penetration by guards often leaves a team without a proper sense of balance. Our concept of balance was explained in the first chapter, but I would like to just re-emphasize two elements of that concept.

One is the balance between inside and outside scoring potential. A team which constantly has its outside men moving inside will find that opponents simply concentrate on stopping the inside game. This will merely make the inside even more congested; whereas, even an occasional outside threat will spread the defense and make the pass and subsequent moves inside much more feasible.

Secondly, the idea of defensive balance has to be considered. With constant penetration from the outside, there is always the danger that no one will be left to guard against the fast break. This is especially true of teams which use one pure guard and send the wing men crashing to the boards for rebounds. One of these wing men may forget to drop back to guard against the fast break if the guard penetrates.

This doesn't mean we never try to penetrate with our outside men. It simply means that on the average, we feel our best outside threats are our perimeter players, and our best inside threats are our pivot men and base-line forwards, and we would like to rely on the percentages. Also, the more you send your outside men inside, the greater danger there is of getting caught off-guard in the transition to defense.

How to Use Versatile Post Positions in Attacking Zones

Since I seem to have gone to some length in emphasizing the importance of the inside game as an entity in itself, it would probably be in order to explain some of the ways in which we try to effect a viable inside attack.

Unlike the previous section, which dealt with a general theoretical approach, perhaps I should first mention that the specific suggestions offered here have proven themselves demonstrably effective in actuality.

In the past five years, we have had two centers (neither of which was over 6′5″) who affected our inside game (two years for one and three years for the other). Both were Conference MVP's (one twice) and both were All-State selections (one twice). Together they scored nearly 3,000 points and hauled down nearly 2,000 rebounds. Together they stand one-two in almost every statistical offensive category in the school's history.

They obviously had great talent, but we would like to think that our system had something significant to do with their success. Having talent is one thing. Implementing it is yet another.

We feel the key to our strong inside attack is the rather wide latitude we offer our inside players in maneuvering for and establishing their position in the area of the foul lane.

Though the term "post man" is used to describe the person playing in this area, it is really a misnomer in our case, for he does not really station himself in a fixed position as a regular assignment. However, the term "post" and "post man" will be used here to describe this area and the personnel maneuvering there.

Basically in a single post attack, which we use most often, we have three post positions which are regularly exploited: the high post (foul line high), the mid-post (midway between the foul line and the basket), and the low post (even with the basket). These positions are the same on either side of the foul lane. So in reality we have seven possible post positions (the high post man may be on either side or in the middle of the lane), and all areas in between. (See Diagram 12-1.)

Our post man may roam in or out of any of these positions at will, unless the situation dictates a more stationary set-up. Each of these positions offers its own separate advantages in terms of causing specific

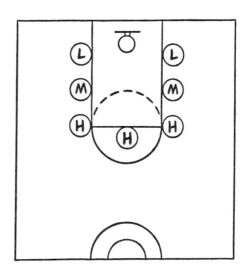

Diagram 12-1

defensive adjustments. By rotating the areas regularly, the defense must constantly keep track of where the post man is and react accordingly. Our goal is simply to "go where they aren't." Our post man is willing to work hard to get open. If the defense isn't as ambitious or can't execute, openings are easily created.

The second phase of our inside attack, which lends additonal versatility, is the speed at which we allow our post man to operate.

In some cases, our post man may stand stationary for a given time or move about almost imperceptibly. At other times he may "float" at half-speed, following the movement of the ball. On other occasions, he may execute what we call a "flash post." This is a full-speed straight cut from one position to another.

The direction of the cuts may even further complicate the picture for the defense. In some cases, we may roll our post in a type of "half moon" and even circular direction (Diagram 12-2). In other cases we may use triangular or V cuts (Diagram 12-3), while Diagram 12-4 shows straight and right-angle cuts. Finally, we have the diagonal cut shown in Diagram 12-5. This flash post is often of this type of cut.

Taken in combination, this variety often makes it impossible for the defense to know with any degree of certainty where our post man will be at any given time, how he will get where he's going, or how fast he gets there.

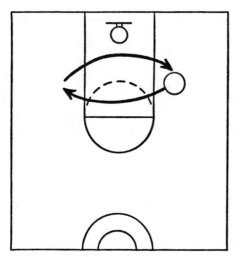

Diagram 12-2

Diagram 12-3

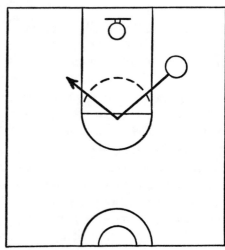

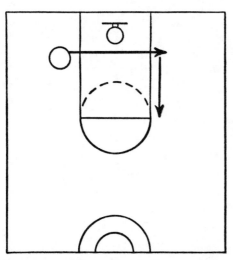

Diagram 12-4

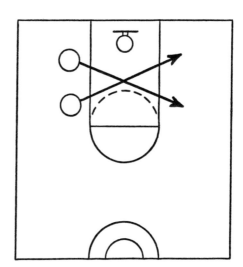

Diagram 12-5

In many cases, the only solution for the defense in keeping the dangerous post man from getting the ball inside is to try to have someone stay with him wherever and whenever he goes. This defeats the basic purpose of a zone, which is to defend by area, not man. It prevents the assigned man from adequately making his proper slides elsewhere.

Where our post man goes, and how he moves, is usually determined by the nature of the defensive personnel. If the opponent has taller, but immobile defenders inside, our post man roams regularly and usually as quickly as possible. If the inside defenders are smaller but quicker, our post man will usually occupy a more stationary position as close to the basket as possible. The particular type of defense and the ability of other defenders to sink and block up the inside will also affect where and how the post man maneuvers.

To further complicate matters for the defense, we may sneak another man (usually a forward) into the post to complement the regular post man (Diagram 12-6). This is especially effective if the inside defenders are overly conscious of the post man and concentrate heavily on him. He may draw undue attention to himself, and the defense may leave other vulnerable areas inside quite open.

I can honestly say that no zone defense has ever totally taken away our inside games, and even when only partial attempts were made to deny the inside games they left other areas so vulnerable that noticeable readjustments to a more normal game were quickly ordered.

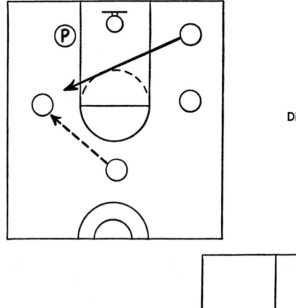

Diagram 12-6

Diagram 12-7

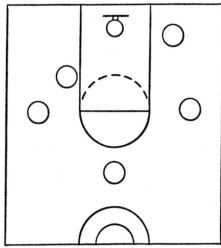

How to Use Multiple Formations in a Zone Attack

As pointed out earlier, these moves are standard for our single post attack. The single post offense used most regularly is the basic 1-3-1 attack shown in Diagram 12-7, as this is the offensive set found to be most universally effective against a variety of zones.

However, there are certain zones which limit the effectiveness of the 1-3-1 offense if it is constantly used. For this reason, we employ a basic component of the Area Key Offense in our zone attack—multiple formations.

Since in our normal 1-3-1 attack, our post man has a variety of position options, each shift in position could easily be constructed by the defense as a different offensive set.

There are other times, however, when we move into definite sets other than the 1-3-1, as they involve more changes than a simple roaming post man. These other sets most commonly used are the 1-2-2, 2-1-2, and 2-2-1 already described in previous chapters. In addition, we also employ a rather nondescriptive arrangement simply known as an overload. This term applies to any set whereby four men occupy one side of the court. Diagrams 12-8 and 12-9 show two possibilities for overloads.

It should also be mentioned that a fundamental aspect of the use of

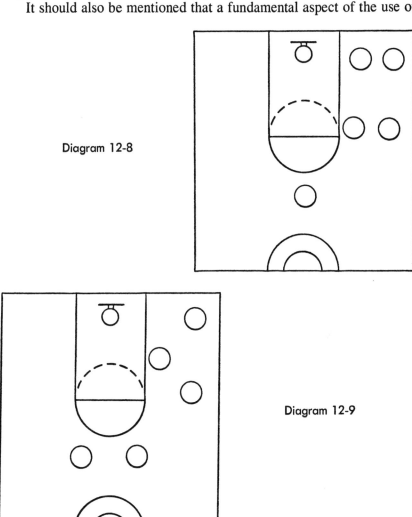

Diagram 12-8

Diagram 12-9

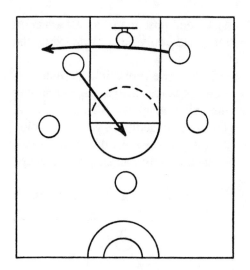

Diagram 12-10

Diagram 12-11

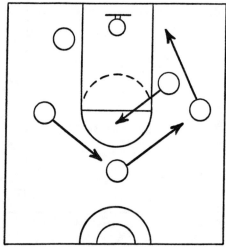

multiple formations in our zone attack is the shifting of sets on any given possession.

Seldom, if ever, do we simply come down the court, assume a given offensive formation, and stay in that formation. In most instances, we shift from one formation into another.

For example, if we plan to go to a 1-3-1 set, we may often start in a 1-2-2 and shift into the 1-3-1 (Diagram 12-10). Or if we plan to try a 2-1-2, we will usually start in a 1-3-1 and rotate into the 2-1-2 (Diagram 12-11).

We feel this shift serves four purposes. First it prevents the defense from drawing a "fix" on our positions and adjusting accordingly. Secondly, whenever a shift occurs, there is the possibility that the defense will not react quickly enough or effectively enough, and an immediate opening may be created just by shifting. In addition, as we shift, the defense may have a tendency to follow us at least partially into our shift, and thereby lose an element of defensive coordination. Lastly, it's very difficult for the defense to "hide" a weak defender or one who is in foul trouble, for eventually he may discover that one of our best offensive threats has found his way into this man's area. This will become clearer when free-lance options are described later.

First, however, it should be explained how different offensive formations can be used to exploit certain weaknesses in the various zone defenses.

Alignments for Various Zones

There are so many basic types of zones and so many individual ways of playing each zone that it's virtually impossible to develop a separate zone offense or set for each zone. To simplify matters for our players, we designate all zones as being one of two varieties—odd front zones and even front zones.

Any zone which presents two defenders at the top of the key is designated as an even front zone (generally the 2-1-2 and 2-3).

Whenever a single front line defender is positioned at the top of the key in the middle of the court, we designate it as an odd front zone (generally the 3-2, 1-2-2, and 1-3-1).

For even front zones, we often like to attack with a single guard (the 1-2-2 or 1-3-1). For odd front zones, we usually try to employ a two-guard offense (2-2-1, 2-1-2).

The overloads may be of either the one- or two-guard variety as shown in Diagrams 12-8 and 12-9.

In essence, what this type of positioning does is allow the offense to split the seams of the defense by positioning some of our men, especially on the perimeter, in between two defenders. This can cause the defender to be uncertain as to who has responsibility for a particular offensive man in the seam or force the defense to have one man cover two consecutive offensive players. Either situation is highly advantageous to the offense.

For example, in Diagram 12-12, O_1 may split X_1 and X_2, creating an opening if neither picks him up directly. If X_1 were to take O_1, he could pass to O_2 who has split the difference between X_1 and X_4 (Diagram 12-13). This would cause some confusion as to whether X_4 should come

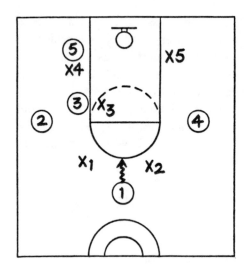

Diagram 12-12

Diagram 12-13

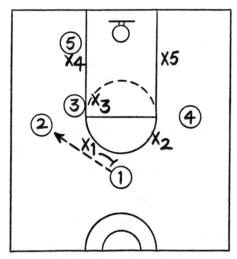

up to cover O_2, for if he does, O_5 may be wide open underneath the basket. This situation may force X_1 to cover both O_1 and O_2 consecutively.

In either case, the defense may be forced to leave a man uncovered or have the defender get there late with the coverage.

The same possibilities occur with a two-guard front against a single-guard offense shown in Diagram 12-14. If X_1 moves over to cover O_1, the ball would be passed to O_2. If X_1 is assigned to cover the entire area at the top of the key, quick ball movement between the two guards should create an eventual opening for either of the guards.

If, on the pass to O_2, X_2 steps up to cover (Diagram 12-15), O_2 would pass to O_4, who steps up into the opening created by X_2 moving out front.

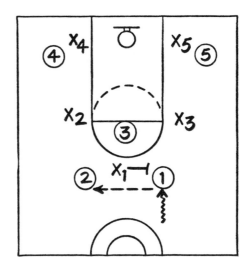

Diagram 12-14

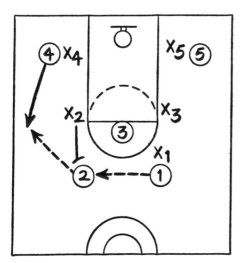

Diagram 12-15

It is not likely that X_2 could recover in time to guard 0_4 also, since he has a bad angle. If X_4 comes out to cover 0_4, an opening would be created underneath for either 0_3 or 0_5 to exploit. A likely offensive move in this case would be to send 0_5 across the base line (Diagram 12-16) and drop 0_3 into the seam in the post. This would create an overload situation mentioned earlier.

One defensive ploy designed to prevent rapid ball movement around the perimeter and stop such openings is to try to cut off the perimeter pass by moving the defenders further out.

Our theory here is quite simple. No team has the ability to cut off both the outside and inside game simultaneously. The court has too many

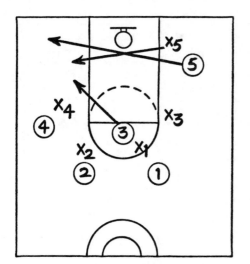

Diagram 12-16

Diagram 12-17

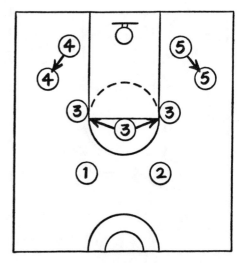

scoring areas, and five men aren't enough to cover them all at once. If a team tries to cut off the perimeter passing lanes, our players are instructed to spread out and then look inside immediately without waiting for any other normal patterns to develop.

Conversely, if the defense sags inside as a primary responsibility, the normal movements on the perimeter should create enough openings there to eventually force the defense to break up the inside concentration.

Free-Lancing in the Zone Offense

On the surface all of this may sound like our Zone Offense is very highly structured and patterned. In actuality, though, if you really look carefully at what has been stated so far, you will see that most of these suggestions are really rather general ones. They offer a basic frame of reference from which to operate much like the Area Key Offense. And, also, like the Area Key Offense, much of our scoring potential comes from simple but basic free-lance maneuvers.

For instance, in regard to formations themselves, they are really not as "cut and dried" as they may appear. A 2-1-2 set may be either tight on the back line or spread wider (Diagram 12-17). In addition, the high post man may be in the middle of the lane or off to one side.

Shifting formations may also call for individual player initiative. In Diagrams 12-18 and 12-19, you see two possible ways of going from a 2-1-2 into a 2-2-1 formation.

Diagram 12-18

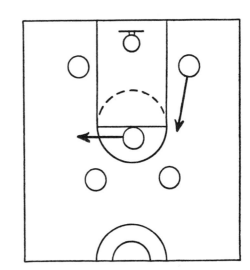

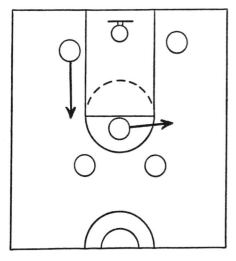

Diagram 12-19

In addition, picking one of the wide number of post positions, cuts, and speeds described earlier is usually left to the discretion of the player involved as to which one he feels is most advantageous.

Specific scouting reports, certain game conditions, or particular personnel requirements may necessitate certain restrictions, but generally our players exercise a good deal of individual freedom.

Many of the individual free-lance moves are based on nothing more than our players' ability to diagnose particular openings and move accordingly within this general structure and pattern of our offense.

In fact, we feel it is essential to the success of any zone defense that players have the freedom and ability to exercise these options. If a perimeter seam is open, and no one enters it, a golden opportunity is lost. The same applies to a lag in coverage in the post area or on the base line.

Special Tactics to Create Openings

On some occasions, however, you will find that your players are either not reacting to definite openings or are failing to create such openings. In these cases, you may be forced to set up some definite pattern if only for structure.

When this situation arises, we have found two specific tactics to be particularly effective. Both involve one simple principle of our zone attack: Force a defender to one extreme of his defensive coverage and then move the ball to the other extreme of his coverage as quickly as possible. If another defender tries to help, look for the vulnerabilities of this defender. A team may compensate on one move, but it can't play "catch up" indefinitely. Sooner or later someone will be left open. However, you still can never be sure of exactly where the opening will occur. But since you are creating the situations, your players have a better idea of where the openings will be.

The first of these special tactics is what we call "the pull." In this play, we try to pull the defender to an extreme of his coverage area on the dribble and then quickly reverse the ball to the other extreme. If another defender tries to help him out, he will be in all likelihood at the extreme of his coverage area. What you may do is force the entire defense to play "catch up" until someone fails to offer the needed help.

In Diagram 12-20, O_1 pulls X_1 to the right wing from a 2-1-2 defense. With X_1 at the extreme of his coverage area, O_1 quickly passes back to O_2. Very rarely could X_1 cover O_2 also. If he tries, we should have an open shot at the top of the foul circle, or closer, if O_2 can dribble in. If

Diagram 12-20

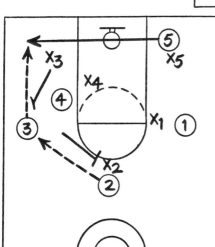

Diagram 12-21

X_2 comes out to cover 0_2, then 0_2 will pass to 0_3 (Diagram 12-21). This would allow the shot from the wing or force X_3 out on 0_3. On this latter move, 0_5 would move across the base line to the extreme of X_3's coverage. X_4 could conceivably cover this pass, but then 0_4 might easily find an opening inside (Diagram 12-22) by dropping down to the other extreme of X_3's coverage. This process would continue, with the ball always being moved as quickly and directly as possible to the other extreme area of coverage of whichever man is guarding the ball, until one defender fails to compensate or recover.

It generally takes only a few passes until the defense fails to execute properly.

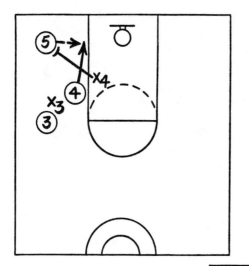

Diagram 12-22

Diagram 12-23

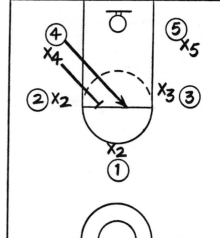

Another way to draw a defender into a position which will make recovery difficult is to "match up" with the defense and then move from this alignment into the extreme area of coverage without the ball. This tactic is the key to our second pattern which we refer to simply as the "match and draw."

By matching originally with the defense, we feel we can create a false sense of security in our opponents since they may feel that their areas of coverage are rather easily defined. Once we begin our movements, the defense is often slow to react at first. Eventually this feeling of predictability is gone, usually after the first few possessions, but we feel there is some minor advantage, at least, in building up hopes and then breaking them down again.

"Drawing" the opponents serves the same basic function as the "pull," except it accomplishes this purpose on the inside rather than on the perimeters.

In Diagram 12-23, the defense is in a 1-2-2 zone defense, and we assume a 1-2-2 offensive alignment. With the ball at the top of the key, O_4 breaks up to the foul line giving us a 1-3-1 set. X_4 must follow or O_4 could easily receive the pass uncontested. As soon as X_4 has been drawn to an extreme of his coverage area, O_5 moves across the base line to a point where X_4 would find it difficult to recover (Diagram 12-24). The ball is then moved quickly to this side. If X_2 tries to cover both O_2 and O_5, he will find it extremely difficult to make the second move at an angle to stop O_5. If X_4 tries to cover O_5 (Diagram 12-25), O_4 would drop to a low post directly and await a base-line pass. X_5, of course, could come over to guard O_4, but then O_3, who has dropped low opposite O_4, might be open. If X_3 drops to an extreme of his coverage area to guard the pass, O_1 should find an opening on the weak side (Diagram 12-26). Rapid ball movement of this sort would not only cause extremes of coverage in designated areas, but may also draw opponents completely out of the assigned coverage areas.

As with any other team, depending upon our personnel from year to year, we find certain zones more troublesome than others. Still, the zone

Diagram 12-24

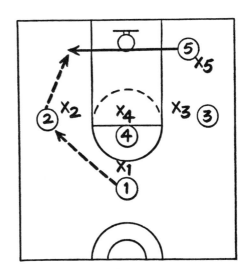

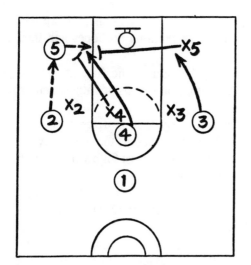

Diagram 12-25

Diagram 12-26

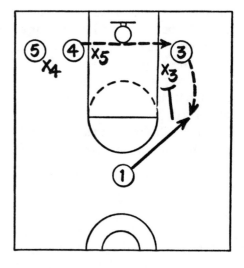

attack described here has generally proven effective in one phase or another regardless of what zones we face or what our personnel are.

However, without wishing to belabor the point, there is still one ultimate weapon against a particularly troublesome zone. Assuming game conditions are right and you make your move at the right time, you may force a team out of the zone and into man-for-man coverage with the tactics described earlier.

Both the zone and man-for-man offenses are designed to be compatible with one another in so many respects that any such transition should present little if any difficulty.

Index